GW00580013

# THE IRISH GRANNY'S
## *pocket*
# FARMHOUSE
# SOUPS

Gill Books
Hume Avenue, Park West, Dublin 12

www.gillbooks.ie

Gill Books is an imprint of M.H. Gill & Co.

Copyright © Teapot Press Ltd 2020

ISBN: 978-0-7171-8601-3

This book was created and produced by Teapot Press Ltd

Recipes compiled by Fiona Biggs
Designed by Tony Potter & Becca Wildman
Photography by Ben Potter
Home economics by Christine Potter

Printed in Europe

This book is typeset in Garamond and Dax

A CIP catalogue record for this book is available
from the British Library.

5 4 3 2 1

# The Irish Granny's *pocket*
# FARMHOUSE
# SOUPS

## Over 100 Homemade Bowls of Comfort

**Fiona Biggs**

**Gill Books**

# Contents

# Introduction

There is almost nothing in the cook's repertoire that is simpler to make or more versatile than soup. The most basic storecupboard ingredients or the contents of the vegetable drawer in the refrigerator can be used to prepare a hearty meal in very little time. A little more effort and a few more ingredients will produce sophisticated results fit for any gourmet occasion. Making your own soup is not only cheaper, it is also healthier. Whether it's a basic mutton broth, a delicate clear soup or a delectable prawn bisque, if you make it from scratch you can be sure that it will contain considerably less salt than any shop-bought variety and absolutely no preservatives.

Our grandmothers would have made soup almost every day, using seasonal ingredients and whatever came to hand. However, with the wide range of readymade soups now available, home preparation has largely fallen by the wayside and we seem to have forgotten just how easy it is to make our own. Vegetables that are less than fresh make great soup ingredients – just put them in a saucepan with some stock and let them simmer for half an hour. If you keep a few cans of tomatoes, chickpeas and lentils in your storecupboard you'll always have the makings of a delicious soup. Most soups can also be bulked out with pasta, rice and barley.

No matter how humble the ingredients, make sure you pay a little attention to the presentation. A swirl of cream, yogurt or pesto, a andful of croûtons, a sprinkling of fresh herbs or citrus zest will make ny bowl of soup look enticing. Some good bread is an indispensable ccompaniment.

The basis of any soup is a good stock, for which there are several cipes in this book. They can all be made in large batches and frozen. using a readymade stock, look for one that is low in salt. Many stock bes and concentrates are very strong, and will interfere with delicate avours, so shop around to find one that suits your taste.

Soup-making requires very little in the way of kitchen equipment, o matter how elaborate a recipe may seem. A large saucepan or ockpot, a chopping board and some good knives, a wooden spoon nd a blender or food processor are essential. Although all the recipes this book specify a food processor, a handheld blender will work just well. A slotted spoon and a sieve would also be useful.

From comforting winter lunchtime soups and hearty soups thick ith ingredients that are a meal in themselves, to refreshing chilled mmer soups and elegant dinner party starters, you'll find a wide range delicious recipes in this book.

Vegan recipes are indicated by this symbol: **Ⓥ**, but many of e other recipes in the book can very easily be adapted to vegan quirements, for example by replacing butter with oil, or chicken stock th vegetable stock.

# MEAT & POULTRY
Meat & Poultry Soups

# Chicken, Leek & Bacon Soup

This hearty soup is prepared using the da[r]
meat of the chicken, giving it a rich flavou[r]
Serve with bread for a substantial main
course.

## INGREDIENTS

1.3 kg/3 lb skinless
chicken thighs
5 celery sticks, finely
sliced
1 onion, roughly
chopped
1 bouquet garni
(bay leaf, parsley
sprigs and tarragon
sprigs)
55 g/2 oz butter
4 leeks, thinly sliced
2 potatoes, diced
150 ml/5 fl oz dry
white wine
1.2 litres/2 pints
chicken stock (see
page 246), plus
extra, if needed
3 tbsp single cream
salt and freshly
ground black pepper
85 g/3 oz crispy
pan-fried lardons, to
garnish

## METHOD

Put the chicken into large saucepan with half the celery, the on[ion]
and the bouquet garni. Add enough water to cover the ingredi[ents]
and bring to the boil.

Reduce the heat, cover and simmer for 1½ hours.

Remove the chicken using a slotted spoon, take the meat off th[e]
bones and set aside. Strain the stock and return it to the sauce[pan.]
Boil over a high heat until it has reduced to 1.5 litres/2¾ pints[.]

Meanwhile, melt the butter in a large, heavy-based saucepan, a[dd]
the leeks and the remaining celery, cover and cook over a low [heat]
for 10 minutes until softened but not browned. Add the potato[es,]
wine and 1.2 litres/2 pints of the stock. Season to taste with
salt and pepper and bring to the boil, then reduce the heat an[d]
simmer for 15 minutes, or until the potatoes are cooked.

Transfer the soup to the bowl of a food processor with the
reserved chicken and process until smooth. If the soup is too
thick, add a little more stock, then stir in the cream and reheat
over a low heat. Do not boil.

Ladle the soup into warmed bowls, garnish with the lardons a[nd]
serve immediately.

SERVES 4-6

## INGREDIENTS

25 g/1 oz butter

1 onion, finely
chopped

1 tbsp plain flour

1.2 litres/2 pints
chicken stock (see
page 246)

100 g/3½ oz fresh
peas

2 tbsp snipped fresh
chives

1 fresh tarragon
sprig, plus extra
to garnish

6 spring onions,
finely chopped

3 chicken breasts,
cut into thin strips

2 eggs

150 ml/5 fl oz single
cream

salt and freshly
ground white pepper

# Balnamoon Skink

This rich chicken soup, made with eggs
and cream, is a complete meal in a bowl.

## METHOD

Heat the butter in a large saucepan over a low heat until
melted. Add the onion and cook for 2–3 minutes until softened
but not browned. Add the flour and stir for 3 minutes, then
gradually stir in the stock. Increase the heat and bring to the
boil, then reduce the heat and simmer for 5 minutes.

Add the peas, chives, tarragon and spring onions and season
to taste with salt and pepper. Add the chicken and cook for 2
minutes, then remove from the heat.

Beat the eggs in a bowl with the cream, add a ladleful of the
soup and stir well. Pour into the soup and reheat, without
boiling, until thickened.

Ladle into warmed bowls, garnish with tarragon and serve
immediately.

**SERVES 6**

## INGREDIENTS

850 ml/1½ pints
chicken stock (see
page 246)
4 boneless, skinless
chicken breasts
55 g/2 oz butter
3 spring onions,
finely chopped
115 g/4 oz smoked
bacon lardons
25 g/1 oz plain flour
450 g/1 lb canned
sweetcorn, drained
300 ml/10 fl oz milk
3 tbsp chopped fresh
parsley
salt and freshly
ground black pepper

# Chicken & Sweetcorn Soup

Chicken and sweetcorn complement each
other perfectly in this soup. The bacon
adds flavour and texture, but do take it
easy with the salt!

## METHOD

Put the stock into a large saucepan and bring to the boil. Add
the chicken and bring back to the boil, then reduce the heat
and simmer for 12–15 minutes until the chicken is cooked
through. Remove the chicken using a slotted spoon and set
aside until cool. Reserve the stock.

Heat the butter in a separate large saucepan over a low heat
until melted. Add the spring onions and cook for 5 minutes, or
until softened. Add the lardons and cook, stirring occasionally,
for 5 minutes, or until beginning to brown. Add the flour and
cook for 1 minute, stirring constantly. Gradually add the stock
and bring to the boil, stirring, until the soup thickens.

Remove from the heat and add the sweetcorn and half the milk.
Return to a medium heat and cook, stirring occasionally, for 5
minutes.

Cut the chicken into bite-sized pieces and add to the soup with
the remaining milk. Bring to the boil and cook for 5 minutes,
then season to taste with salt and pepper, stir in the parsley and
serve immediately in warmed bowls.

SERVES 4

## INGREDIENTS

4 tbsp olive oil
1 onion, thinly sliced
2 garlic cloves, crushed
2 red peppers, cored, deseeded and cut into short strips
4 skinless, boneless chicken breasts
6 tbsp tomato purée
3 potatoes, diced
3 tsp chopped fresh mixed herbs
3 carrots, cut into small pieces
2 courgettes, sliced
salt and freshly ground black pepper
chopped fresh herbs, to garnish

# Chicken Soup with Mediterranean Vegetables

While the peppers and carrots benefit from a longer cooking time, don't add the courgettes too soon or they will become mushy.

## METHOD

Heat the oil in a large saucepan. Add the onion and garlic and cook for 1–2 minutes until softened. Add the red peppers and cook for a further 3 minutes.

Put the chicken breasts into the saucepan and brown them, turning, for 10 minutes.

Add the tomato purée, potatoes, herbs and carrots with enough water to just cover, and season to taste with salt and pepper. Cover and cook over a low heat for about 40–50 minutes.

Add the courgettes 5 minutes before the end of cooking. Remove the chicken breasts with a slotted spoon and cut them into bite-sized pieces, then return to the soup.

Ladle the soup into warmed bowls, garnish with herbs and serve immediately.

**SERVES 4**

## INGREDIENTS

1 duck carcass
1 large onion
2 carrots, cut into large chunks
1 parsnip, cut into large chunks
1 leek, cut into large chunks
4 garlic cloves, crushed
2.5-cm/1-inch piece fresh ginger, peeled and thinly sliced
1 tbsp whole black peppercorns
bouquet garni (thyme sprigs, coriander sprigs)

# Clear Duck Soup

This soup is a great way to use a duck carcass left over from another meal and makes a light starter. Don't push the soup through the sieve, or the consommé will be cloudy.

## METHOD

Put all the ingredients into a large saucepan, cover with cold water and bring to the boil, skimming off any scum that rises to the surface.

Reduce the heat to low and simmer for 2 hours, then strain into a large bowl through a sieve lined with muslin. Leave the stock to cool, then chill overnight.

Remove the fat that will have formed on top of the liquid (the liquid will have taken on a jelly-like consistency). Put the jelly into a saucepan and reheat over a medium heat. Do not boil.

Ladle into warmed bowls and serve immediately.

**SERVES 4**

## INGREDIENTS

450 g/1 lb lean neck of lamb, diced

280 g/10 oz carrots, diced

175 g/6 oz onions, diced

2 leeks, sliced

1 white turnip, diced

2 tbsp pearl barley

1.7 litres/3 pints water

salt and freshly ground black pepper

finely chopped fresh parsley, to serve

# Mutton Broth

This traditional soup is very substantial and is usually served as a main course.

## METHOD

Put the meat, carrots, onions, leeks, turnip and barley into a large saucepan. Season to taste with plenty of salt and pepper and add the water.

Cover and bring to the boil over a medium heat, then reduce the heat and simmer for 1½–2 hours.

Stir in the parsley and serve in warmed bowls.

**SERVES 6**

## INGREDIENTS

1 bacon hock, weighing 900 g/ 2 lb, soaked in cold water overnight, drained
85 g/3 oz pearl barley
85 g/3 oz red lentils
2 leeks, thickly sliced
4 carrots, diced
200 g/7 oz turnip, diced
3 potatoes, diced
bouquet garni (bay leaf, thyme sprig, parsley sprig)
1 small Savoy cabbage, trimmed, cored and sliced
freshly ground black pepper
chopped fresh parsley, to garnish

# Bacon & Barley Soup

This comforting main course soup is a great winter warmer. The bacon is very salty, so don't add extra salt.

## METHOD

Put the bacon into a large saucepan, cover with cold water and bring to the boil. Skim off any scum that has risen to the surface and add the barley and lentils. Bring back to the boil, then reduce the heat and simmer for 15 minutes.

Add the leeks, carrots, turnip, potatoes and bouquet garni, season to taste with pepper and bring back to the boil. Reduce the heat and simmer for 1½–2 hours until the bacon is tender.

Remove and discard the bouquet garni. Take the bacon out of the saucepan with a slotted spoon, remove the skin and pull the meat away from the bones. Cut into small cubes and return to the saucepan. Add the cabbage and cook for 5 minutes, or until the cabbage is cooked to your liking.

Ladle into warmed bowls, garnish with parsley and serve immediately.

SERVES 6

## INGREDIENTS

2 tbsp vegetable oil
600 g/1 lb 5 oz beef kidney, skinned, cored and sliced
2 tbsp flour
2 litres/3½ pints beef stock (see page 252)
1 tbsp sugar
bouquet garni (bay leaf, thyme sprigs, parsley sprigs)
1 tsp fresh lemon juice
125 ml/4 fl oz sherry
salt and freshly ground black pepper
croûtons (see page 224) and fresh flatleaf parsley sprigs, to garnish

# Kidney Soup

## A beefy soup that is full of goodness and subtle flavours.

### METHOD

Heat the oil in a large saucepan, then add the meat and cook, turning occasionally, until browned all over. Drain the excess fat, then stir in the flour and cook for 1 minute.

Add the stock, sugar and bouquet garni. Bring to the boil, the reduce the heat, cover and simmer for about 3 hours.

Leave to cool, then chill in the refrigerator. Remove and disca the bouquet garni and skim the fat from the surface of the so

Season to taste with salt and pepper, add the lemon juice and sherry and process in a food processor. Transfer to a clean saucepan and heat until piping hot. Do not boil. Ladle into warmed bowls, garnish with croûtons and parsley sprigs and serve immediately.

**SERVES 6**

## INGREDIENTS

450 g/1 lb stewing
beef, cubed

2 onions, roughly
chopped

55 g/2 oz pearl
barley

55 g/2 oz green
split peas

2 litres/3½ pints
beef stock (see page
252)

4 carrots, roughly
chopped

2 white turnips,
diced

3 celery sticks,
chopped

2 leeks, thinly sliced

salt and freshly
ground black pepper

# Beef & Barley Soup

The flavours in this soup really improve
if it is left overnight and reheated before
serving.

## METHOD

Put the beef into a large saucepan with the onions, barley
and split peas, add the stock and season to taste with salt and
pepper. Bring to the boil, skimming off any scum that rises to
the surface. Reduce the heat, cover and simmer for 30 minute

Add the remaining vegetables and simmer for a further 1 hou
or until the beef is tender.

Ladle into warmed bowls and serve immediately after heating

**SERVES 6**

## INGREDIENTS

1 tbsp vegetable oil

4 skinless, boneless chicken breasts, cut into bite-sized pieces

150 g/5½ oz smoked bacon lardons

3 carrots, thinly sliced

2 leeks, thickly sliced

1.2 litres/2 pints chicken stock (see page 246)

salt and freshly ground black pepper

# Cock-a-Leekie

**The smoked bacon adds extra flavour to this traditional Scottish soup. This versio: is very quick and easy to prepare.**

## METHOD

Heat the oil in a large heavy-based saucepan over a medium heat. Add the chicken in batches and fry until golden brown, then remove from the saucepan and set aside.

Add the bacon, carrots and leeks to the saucepan and fry unti softened but not browned. Return the chicken to the saucepa and add the stock, salt and peper. Bring to the boil, then red the heat and simmer for 20 minutes until the chicken is tend

Ladle into warmed bowls and serve immediately.

**SERVES 4–6**

# SMOOTH & CREAMY

Smooth & Creamy Soups

## INGREDIENTS

115 g/4 oz butter
1 kg/2 lb 4 oz white
onions, thinly sliced
1 bay leaf
100 ml/3½ fl oz dry
white vermouth
1 litre/1¾ pints
chicken stock (see
page 246)
150 ml/5 fl oz
double cream
salt and freshly
ground black pepper
croûtons (see page
224) and fresh basil
sprigs to garnish

**SERVES 4–6**

# Creamy Onion Soup with Vermout

## The onions are cooked down in butter and vermouth to make a wonderfully mellow soup.

### METHOD

Heat two-thirds of the butter in a large saucepan over a low heat until melted. Reserve 250g/8 oz of the onions and add th remainder to the saucepan with the bay leaf, stirring to coat ir the butter. Cover and cook for 30 minutes until the onions ar very soft but not browned.

Add the vermouth, increase the heat and bring to the boil. Bo rapidly until the vermouth has evaporated. Add the stock with salt and pepper to taste and bring to the boil, then reduce the heat to low and simmer for about 5 minutes.

Remove from the heat and leave to cool. Remove and discard the bay leaf, transfer the soup to the bowl of a food processor and process until smooth. Return the soup to the saucepan.

Meanwhile, put the remaining butter into a separate saucepa and heat until melted. Add the reserved onions, cover and co over a low heat until softened but not browned. Continue to cook, uncovered, until the onions are golden.

Add the cream to the processed soup and reheat over a low heat, making sure that it doesn't boil. Add the onions and stir for 1 minute, then ladle the soup into warmed bowls. Garnis with croûtons and basil sprigs and serve immediately.

# Cream of Parsnip Soup

The humble parsnip comes into its own i
this thick and creamy soup, which is give
added interest with the inclusion of subt
spices.

## INGREDIENTS

55 g/2 oz butter
1 kg/2 lb 4 oz
parsnips, peeled and
thinly sliced
1 onion, finely
chopped
2 garlic cloves, finely
chopped
2 tsp ground cumin
1 tsp ground
coriander
1.2 litres/2 pints
vegetable or chicken
stock (see pages
244/246)
150 ml/5 fl oz single
cream
salt and freshly
ground black pepper
croûtons (see page
224) and fresh
parsley sprigs, to
garnish

## METHOD

Heat the butter in a large saucepan over a medium heat until
melted. Add the parsnips, onion and garlic and cook until
beginning to soften.

Add the spices and cook for a further 1–2 minutes, then
gradually add the stock and bring to the boil, stirring constan

Reduce the heat, cover and simmer for 15–20 minutes until
parsnips are very soft.

Transfer the soup to the bowl of a food processor and proces
until smooth.

Return to the saucepan, add the cream and season to taste w
salt and pepper, then reheat over a low heat. Do not boil.

Serve immediately in warmed bowls, garnished with croûton
and parsley.

**SERVES 6**

## INGREDIENTS

25 g/1 oz butter

3 spring onions, finely chopped

700 g/1 lb 9 oz shelled fresh peas

¼ tsp sugar

1.2 litres/2 pints vegetable stock (see page 244)

2 tbsp fresh mint leaves

450 g/1 lb baby spinach leaves

150 ml/5 fl oz double cream

salt and freshly ground black pepper

fresh mint sprigs, to garnish

# Minted Pea Soup with Spinach

This smooth green soup is prepared with young and tender spring vegetables.

## METHOD

Heat the butter in a large saucepan over a low heat until melted. Add the spring onions and cook, stirring, for 5 minut until softened.

Add the peas, sugar, stock and half the mint leaves. Increase the heat and bring to the boil, then reduce the heat, cover an simmer for 10 minutes until the peas are soft. Add the spinac and stir until wilted.

Remove from the heat and leave to cool. Add the remaining mint, transfer to the bowl of a food processor and process ur smooth. Return the soup to the saucepan.

Season to taste with salt and pepper, stir in the cream, then reheat over a low heat. Do not boil.

To serve, ladle into six warmed bowls and garnish with mint sprigs.

**SERVES 6**

## INGREDIENTS

25 g/1 oz butter
1 large onion, finely chopped
450 g/1 lb butternut squash flesh
1.2 litres/2 pints vegetable stock (see page 244)
225 g/8 oz potatoes, diced
¼ tsp ground cumin
125 ml/4 fl oz canned coconut milk
salt and freshly ground black pepper
snipped fresh chives or chopped fresh parsley, to garnish

# Butternut Squash Soup

The earthy flavour of the butternut squas is complemented by the creamy coconut milk that is added towards the end of cooking.

## METHOD

Heat the butter in a large saucepan over a low heat until melted. Add the onion and cook, stirring, for 5 minutes until softened but not browned.

Add the squash, stock, potatoes and cumin, increase the heat to medium and bring to the boil. Reduce the heat to low, cov and simmer for 30 minutes, or until the squash and potatoes are soft.

Transfer the soup to the bowl of a food processor and proces until smooth. Return to the saucepan and add the coconut milk. Season to taste with salt and pepper and reheat over a l heat. Do not boil.

Ladle the soup into warmed bowls, garnish with chives and serve immediately.

**SERVES 4-6**

## INGREDIENTS

25 g/1 oz butter
1 onion, finely chopped
1 carrot, finely chopped
1 celery stick, finely chopped
1 garlic clove, finely chopped
900 g/2 lb canned chopped tomatoes
2 tsp sugar
600 ml/1 pint chicken stock (see page 246)
1 tbsp chopped fresh basil
600 ml/1 pint milk
salt and freshly ground black pepper
single cream, to garnish

# Traditional Tomato Soup

You need tomatoes with a really good flavour for this soup, so unless you live in a Mediterranean climate, your best option is to use canned tomatoes.

## METHOD

Heat the butter in a large saucepan over a medium heat until melted. Add the onion, carrot, celery and garlic and cook, stirring, for 5 minutes, or until softened and just beginning to brown.

Add the tomatoes, sugar, stock and basil and bring to the boil, then cover, reduce the heat and simmer for 20 minutes.

Remove from the heat, transfer to the bowl of a food processor and process until smooth, then pass through a non-metallic sieve to remove the tomato seeds. Return to the saucepan, add the milk and heat, stirring. Do not boil.

Season to taste with salt and pepper and ladle into warmed bowls. Garnish with swirls of cream and serve immediately.

**SERVES 6**

## INGREDIENTS

4 tbsp olive oil

1 small butternut squash, peeled, deseeded and cut into chunks

1 small swede, peeled and cut into chunks

2 carrots, thickly sliced

1 large parsnip, peeled and cut into chunks

2 leeks, thickly sliced

1 onion, cut into quarters

4 bay leaves

4 fresh thyme sprigs

4 fresh rosemary sprigs

1.2 litres/2 pints vegetable stock (see page 244)

salt and freshly ground black pepper

single cream and fresh thyme sprigs, to garnish

**SERVES 6**

# Roasted Winter Vegetable Soup

Roasting vegetables is guaranteed to add wonderful depth of flavour and adds interest to this classic winter warmer.

## METHOD

Preheat the oven to 200°C/400°F/Gas Mark 6.

Put the oil into a large bowl, add all the vegetables and toss to coat thoroughly.

Spread the vegetables in the base of a large roasting tin in a single layer, tucking in the bay leaves, thyme and rosemary.

Roast in the preheated oven for 50 minutes, or until tender, turning occasionally. Discard the herbs and transfer the vegetables to a large saucepan.

Add the stock and bring to the boil over a medium heat, then reduce the heat and simmer for about 10 minutes. Transfer to the bowl of a food processor and process until smooth.

Return to the saucepan and heat through. Do not boil. Season to taste and ladle into warmed bowls, then garnish with cream and thyme sprigs and serve immediately.

## INGREDIENTS

25 g/1 oz butter
1 onion, finely
chopped
1 garlic clove, finely
chopped
450 g/1 lb button
mushrooms, chestnut
mushrooms or a
mixture
1 tbsp plain flour
850 ml/1½ pints
vegetable stock (see
page 244)
150 ml/5 fl oz
double cream, plus
extra to garnish
salt and freshly
ground black pepper
fried mushroom
slices, to garnish

# Cream of Mushroom Soup

This creamy classic is an all-time favourite
You could add a dash of sherry just before
serving for a touch of luxury.

## METHOD

Heat the butter in a large saucepan over a medium heat until
melted. Add the onion and garlic and cook for 5 minutes until
softened but not browned. Add the mushrooms, cover and
cook for 10 minutes, stirring occasionally.

Add the flour, stir and cook for 1 minute. Add the stock and
bring to the boil, then reduce the heat and simmer for 10–15
minutes.

Remove from the heat and leave to cool, then pour into the
bowl of a food processor and process until smooth.

Return the soup to the saucepan and add the cream, season to
taste with salt and pepper, stir well and reheat over a medium
heat. Do not boil.

Ladle the soup into warmed bowls, garnish each portion with
a swirl of cream and some fried mushroom slices and serve
immediately.

SERVES 6

## INGREDIENTS

4 tbsp olive oil

1 cauliflower, divided into florets

2 large onions, finely chopped

1 garlic clove, finely chopped

3 large potatoes, diced

2 celery sticks, finely chopped

1.7 litres/3 pints chicken stock (see page 246)

2 carrots, finely chopped

1 tbsp chopped fresh parsley

1 tbsp lemon juice

300 ml/10 fl oz single cream

salt and freshly ground black pepper

croûtons (see page 224) and fresh parsley sprigs, to garnish

**SERVES 6**

# Cream of Cauliflower Soup

Roasting the cauliflower adds great depth of flavour to this satisfying soup.

## METHOD

Preheat the oven to 180°C/350°F/Gas Mark 4. Put 2 tablespoons of the oil into a large bowl, add the cauliflower florets and turn to coat. Arrange the florets on a baking tray in a single layer and roast in the preheated oven for 30 minutes.

Meanwhile, heat the remaining oil in a large saucepan over a medium heat. Add the onions and garlic and cook, stirring occasionally, until softened but not browned. Add the potatoes, celery and stock and bring to the boil, then reduce the heat and simmer for 10 minutes. Add the carrots and simmer for a further 10 minutes.

Add the roasted cauliflower, parsley and lemon juice and simmer for a further 20 minutes, or until all the vegetables are tender.

Transfer the soup to the bowl of a food processor and process until smooth. Return to the saucepan, season to taste with salt and pepper, stir in the cream and reheat over a low heat.

To serve, ladle into warmed bowls and garnish with croûtons and parsley sprigs.

## INGREDIENTS

2 tbsp olive oil
2 garlic cloves, finely chopped
2 tbsp finely chopped fresh basil
1 kg/2 lb 4 oz courgettes, cut into 1-cm/½-inch slices
700 ml/1¼ pints vegetable stock (see page 244)
100 ml/3½ fl oz milk
55 g/2 oz grated Parmesan cheese, plus extra to serve
salt and freshly ground black pepper
croûtons (see page 224) and snipped fresh chives, to garnish

# Creamy Courgette Soup

This unusual soup is light and fresh – you could replace half the milk with single cream for a creamier finish.

## METHOD

Heat the oil in a large saucepan over a medium heat. Add the garlic, basil and courgettes, season to taste with salt and cook for 10 minutes until the courgettes are soft.

Add the stock and simmer for 5 minutes, uncovered, then add the milk and bring just to simmering. Season to taste with pepper.

Transfer the soup to a food processor and process until smooth, then return to the pan and stir in the cheese.

Ladle the soup into warmed bowls, garnish with croûtons and chives and serve immediately. Add extra Parmesan cheese to taste.

**SERVES 4**

## INGREDIENTS

55 g/2 oz butter
3 leeks, sliced
450 g/1 lb carrots, thinly sliced
juice and grated rind of 2 oranges
1.2 litres/2 pints chicken stock (see page 246)
½ tsp freshly grated nutmeg
150 g/5½ oz Greek-style natural yogurt
salt and freshly ground black pepper
fresh coriander sprigs, to garnish

# Summer Carrot Soup

This refreshing soup gets its creaminess from yogurt rather than cream. Zesty orange brings out the flavour of the carrots.

## METHOD

Heat the butter in a large saucepan over a medium heat until melted. Add the leeks and carrots and stir well to coat in the butter. Cover and cook for 10–15 minutes until the vegetables are just beginning to soften.

Add the orange juice and rind and the stock. Add the nutmeg and season to taste with salt and pepper, then bring to the boil over a high heat. Reduce the heat and simmer for 40 minutes, or until the vegetables are very tender.

Transfer the soup to the bowl of a food processor and process until smooth. Return to the saucepan, add the yogurt and reheat over a low heat. Do not boil.

Ladle the soup into warmed bowls, garnish with coriander sprigs and serve immediately.

**SERVES 4**

# PEAS, BEANS & LENTILS

Soups with Peas, Beans & Lentils

## INGREDIENTS

4 tbsp olive oil

1 onion, thinly sliced

4 garlic cloves, crushed

1 carrot, very finely chopped

400 g/14 oz canned chopped tomatoes

1 tbsp tomato purée

½ tsp dried oregano

1 litre/1¾ pints hot vegetable stock (see page 244)

300 g/10½ oz canned lentils, rinsed and drained

4 tbsp sweet chilli sauce

salt and freshly ground black pepper

fresh parsley sprigs, to garnish

# Tomato & Lentil Soup Ⓥ

The sweet chilli sauce adds a kick to this wholesome soup. It's much better when prepared with canned rather than fresh tomatoes.

## METHOD

Put the oil into a large saucepan, then add the onion and cook, stirring, until translucent. Add the garlic and cook for 1 minute, then add the carrot, tomatoes, tomato purée and oregano. Stir in the stock and season to taste with salt and pepper.

Bring to the boil, then reduce the heat and cook for 15–20 minutes. Add the lentils and heat through.

Stir in the sweet chilli sauce and season to taste with salt. Ladle into warmed bowls, garnish with parsley sprigs and serve immediately.

**SERVES 4**

## INGREDIENTS

4 tbsp olive oil

6 garlic cloves, finely sliced

1 onion, finely chopped

800 g/1 lb 12 oz canned chickpeas, rinsed and drained

2 fresh thyme sprigs

juice of 1 lemon

salt and freshly ground black pepper

extra virgin olive oil, for drizzling

chopped fresh parsley, to garnish

# Garlicky Chickpea Soup Ⓥ

This delicious soup is based on a traditional Italian recipe for a pulse-based hearty winter zuppa.

## METHOD

Heat the olive oil in a large saucepan over a low heat, then add the garlic and cook for 5 minutes until softened but not browned. Add the onion and cook for 5 minutes until softened.

Add the chickpeas, reserving 200 g/7 oz, and stir to coat in the oil. Add the thyme and pour in enough hot water to cover the chickpeas. Season to taste with salt and pepper.

Bring to the boil, then reduce the heat and simmer for 30 minutes. Remove and discard the thyme.

Meanwhile, put the reserved chickpeas into the bowl of a food processor and process until mashed. Stir them into the soup with the lemon juice.

Ladle into warmed bowls, drizzle with extra virgin olive oil, garnish with parsley and serve immediately.

SERVES 4-6

# Bean & Vegetable Soup with Pesto

This soup can be made with any bean – borlotti beans are traditional, but can be hard to find, so haricot beans make a good substitute.

## INGREDIENTS

3 tbsp olive oil

2 onions, finely chopped

6 garlic cloves, finely chopped

2 carrots, thinly sliced

2 celery sticks, thinly sliced

1 fennel bulb, trimmed and finely chopped

2 courgettes, sliced

400 g/14 oz canned chopped tomatoes

3 tbsp pesto (see page 240), plus extra to garnish

900 ml/1½ pints vegetable stock (see page 244)

400 g/14 oz canned haricot beans, rinsed and drained

½ tsp dried oregano

salt and freshly ground black pepper

extra virgin olive oil, for drizzling

**SERVES 6**

## METHOD

Heat the olive oil in a large saucepan over a low heat. Add the onions, garlic, carrots, celery and fennel and fry for 10 minutes. Add the courgettes and fry for a further 2 minutes.

Add the tomatoes, pesto, stock, beans and oregano and bring to the boil. Reduce the heat and simmer for 30 minutes, or until all the vegetables are completely tender. Season to taste with salt and pepper.

Ladle into warmed bowls, drizzle with extra virgin olive oil, garnish with pesto and serve immediately.

## INGREDIENTS

25 g/1 oz butter
1 onion, finely chopped
1 potato, diced
1 litre/1¾ pints ham stock (see page 250)
500 g/1 lb 2 oz frozen peas
300 g/10½ oz lean cooked ham, diced
croûtons (see page 224), to garnish

# Pea & Ham Soup

This is a classic winter soup – peas and ham work really well together, and the ham stock makes all the difference to the flavour.

## METHOD

Heat the butter in a large saucepan over a medium heat until foaming. Add the onion and cook for 5–6 minutes until soft. Add the potato and stir to coat in the butter.

Add the stock and simmer, uncovered, until the potato is soft. Add the peas and bring to the boil. Cook for 1–2 minutes, then transfer the soup to the bowl of a food processor and process until smooth. Stir in the ham.

Ladle the soup into warmed bowls, garnish with croûtons and serve immediately.

SERVES 4

## INGREDIENTS

800 g/1 lb 12 oz canned chopped tomatoes

400 ml/14 fl oz water

250 g/9 oz Savoy cabbage leaves, roughly shredded

400 g/14 oz canned cannellini beans, rinsed and drained

½ tsp dried oregano

½ tsp dried thyme

2 tbsp pesto (see page 240)

salt and freshly ground pepper

# Cabbage & Cannellini Bean Sou

Using canned tomatoes and beans mean: that this soup can be prepared in less th; half an hour.

## METHOD

Put the tomatoes into a large saucepan with the water, season to taste with salt and pepper and bring to the boil, then redu the heat and simmer for 5 minutes. Add the cabbage leaves and continue to simmer for 15 minutes, or until the cabbage tender.

Add the beans, oregano and thyme and continue to simmer a further 5 minutes until the beans are warmed through.

Ladle the soup into warmed bowls, drizzle with pesto and se immediately.

SERVES 4

## INGREDIENTS

2 tbsp olive oil

2 onions, finely chopped

4 potatoes, diced

450 g/1 lb fresh shelled baby broad beans

1.7 litres/3 pints vegetable stock (see page 244)

1 bunch fresh flatleaf parsley, roughly chopped, and sprigs to garnish

150 ml/5 fl oz single cream, plus extra to garnish

salt and freshly ground black pepper

# Baby Broad Bean & Potato Soup

This soup works best with really fresh baby broad beans. If they're unavailable, use fresh or frozen peas instead.

## METHOD

Heat the oil in a large saucepan over a low heat. Add the onions and fry, stirring, until softened but not browned.

Add the potatoes, beans and stock and bring to the boil over medium heat. Reduce the heat and simmer for 5 minutes, then add the parsley and simmer for a further 5–10 minutes.

Transfer the soup to the bowl of a food processor and process until smooth, then return to the saucepan and reheat, stirring constantly. Do not boil. Stir in the cream and heat through, then remove from the heat and season to taste with salt and pepper.

Ladle the soup into warmed bowls, garnish with cream and parsley and serve immediately.

SERVES 4

## INGREDIENTS

3 tbsp olive oil
1 onion, finely chopped
8–10 garlic cloves, finely chopped
2 celery sticks, finely chopped
2 carrots, finely chopped
1 potato, diced
250 g/9 oz red lentils
1 litre/1¾ pints vegetable stock (see page 244)
juice of 2 lemons
2 bay leaves
¼ tsp cumin seeds
pinch of paprika
salt and freshly ground black pepper
fresh coriander sprigs, to garnish

# Thick Lentil & Vegetable Soup ♥

## This zesty soup simply bursts with delicious garlicky flavour.

### METHOD

Heat the oil in a large saucepan over a low heat. Add the onion and cook for 5–10 minutes, or until softened but not browned. Add the remaining vegetables and cook for several minutes until beginning to soften.

Add the lentils and stock, increase the heat and bring to the boil, then reduce the heat and simmer for 30 minutes until the potatoes and lentils are tender.

Add the lemon juice, bay leaves and cumin seeds and cook for a further 10 minutes.

Remove and discard the bay leaves, transfer the soup to the bowl of a food processor and process until smooth. Return to the saucepan, add the paprika and season to taste with salt and pepper.

Ladle the soup into warmed bowls, garnish with coriander and serve immediately.

SERVES 4

## INGREDIENTS

3 tbsp olive oil

1 large onion, very finely chopped

3 garlic cloves, very finely chopped

2 carrots, very finely chopped

1 celery stick, very finely chopped

1.2 litres/2 pints hot water

450 g/1 lb shelled fresh peas

225 g/8 oz shelled baby broad beans

3 tomatoes, peeled and roughly chopped

55 g/2 oz soup pasta, such as ditalini

225 g/8 oz baby spinach leaves

handful of fresh parsley sprigs, chopped

salt and freshly grund black pepper

handful of fresh basil leaves, torn

SERVES 6

# Summer Minestrone Ⓥ

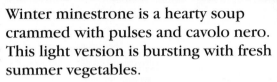

**Winter minestrone is a hearty soup crammed with pulses and cavolo nero. This light version is bursting with fresh summer vegetables.**

## METHOD

Heat the oil in a large saucepan over a low heat. Add the onion and garlic and cook over a low heat for 5 minutes, or until softened but not browned.

Add the carrots and celery and cook for a further 3 minutes, then a the water, bring to the boil and simmer for 15 minutes.

Meanwhile, bring two medium saucepans of lightly salted water to the boil, add the peas to one and the broad beans to the other and cook for 1 minute, until just tender. Drain and refresh under cold water.

Add the tomatoes to the soup and cook for 1 minute. Transfer 250 ml/9 fl oz of the soup to the bowl of a food processor, add a hand of the broad beans and process until smooth. Set aside until need

Add the pasta to the soup and cook for the time specified on the packet until tender but still firm to the bite. Add the broad bean purée and spinach and cook until the spinach is just wilted. Add t remaining broad beans, the peas and the parsley and season to tas with salt and pepper.

Stir the basil into the soup, then ladle into warmed bowls and ser immediately.

## INGREDIENTS

1 tbsp vegetable oil

1 onion, chopped

2 celery sticks, chopped

1 garlic clove, peeled and crushed

1.2 litres/2 pints water

225 g/8 oz dried marrowfat peas, soaked in water and bicarbonate of soda overnight and drained

bouquet garni (bay leaf, thyme sprigs, parsley sprigs)

fresh flatleaf parsley sprigs, to garnish

# Pea Soup Ⓥ

This traditional Irish recipe uses dried marrowfat peas. They need to be soaked overnight with a little bicarbonate of soda

## METHOD

Heat the oil in a large saucepan over a medium heat, add the onion and cook until browned. Add the celery and garlic and cook for about 5 minutes.

Add the water, peas and bouquet garni, bring to the boil, then reduce the heat and simmer for about 2½ hours. Remove from the heat, then remove and discard the bouquet garni.

Transfer the soup to the bowl of a food processor and process until smooth. Return to the saucepan and reheat over a low heat. Serve in warmed bowls, garnished with parsley.

SERVES 8

## INGREDIENTS

800 g/1 lb 12 oz
canned butter beans,
rinsed and drained
900 ml/1½ pints
vegetable stock (see
page 244)
4 tbsp tomato purée
5 tbsp pesto (see
page 240)
salt and freshly
ground black pepper
fresh flatleaf parsley
sprigs, to garnish

# Butter Bean Soup

This soup can be prepared very quickly,
using basic storecupboard ingredients.
You'll have it on the table in less than hal
an hour.

## METHOD

Put the beans into a large saucepan with the stock and bring t
the boil over a high heat.

Reduce the heat and stir in the tomato purée and pesto, then
simmer for 5 minutes.

Transfer the soup to the bowl of a food processor and process
until smooth, then return to the saucepan and reheat over a
low heat. Season to taste with salt and pepper.

Ladle into four warmed bowls, garnish with parsley and serve
immediately.

**SERVES 4**

**VEGETARIAN**
Vegetarian Soups

## INGREDIENTS

55 g/2 oz butter

1 onion, finely chopped

55 g/2 oz plain flour

1.2 litres/2 pints milk

150 g/5½ oz mature vegetarian Cheddar cheese, coarsely grated, plus extra to serve

1 celeriac, cut into small chunks

salt and freshly ground black pepper

chopped fresh parsley, to garnish

# Celeriac Soup with Cheddar Cheese

This recipe combines the sharp flavour of mature Cheddar cheese with the nutty sweetness of celeriac.

## METHOD

Heat the butter in a large saucepan over a low heat until melted. Add the onion and cook, stirring occasionally, until softened but not browned.

Sprinkle in the flour and cook, stirring, for 2 minutes, then slowly add the milk, stirring well after each addition.

Continue to cook, stirring constantly, until the mixture begins to thicken. Add one third of the cheese and cook, stirring occasionally, for 5 minutes.

Meanwhile, bring a saucepan of water to the boil, add the celeriac, bring back to the boil and cook for 10 minutes until tender. Drain and add to the soup with the remaining cheese and stir until the cheese has melted completely.

Season to taste with salt and pepper, then ladle into warmed bowls, garnish with parsley and serve immediately with some grated cheese on the side.

SERVES 4

## INGREDIENTS

350 g/12 oz mixed mushrooms, chopped

4 celery sticks, chopped

4 garlic cloves, finely chopped

2 potatoes, diced

700 ml/1¼ pints vegetable stock (see page 244)

pinch of paprika

salt and freshly ground black pepper

chopped fresh parsley, to garnish

# Mushroom & Celery Soup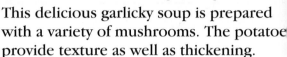

This delicious garlicky soup is prepared with a variety of mushrooms. The potatoes provide texture as well as thickening.

## METHOD

Put the mushrooms, celery, garlic and potatoes into a large saucepan with 200 ml/9 fl oz of the stock and bring to the boil. Reduce the heat and simmer for 30–40 minutes until the potatoes are tender.

Transfer to the bowl of a food processor with a little more stock and process until smooth. Return to the saucepan, stir in the remaining stock and the paprika and bring to the boil. Season to taste with salt and pepper, then ladle into warmed bowls, garnish with parsley and serve immediately.

**SERVES 4**

## INGREDIENTS

25 g/1 oz butter
450 g/1 lb parsnips, peeled and sliced
1 Bramley apple, peeled and chopped
1.2 litres/2 pints vegetable stock (see page 244)
½ tsp dried sage
2 cloves
single or double cream, to garnish
chopped fresh parsley, to garnish

# Parsnip & Apple Soup

This fresh-tasting soup makes the most of autumnal garden produce.

## METHOD

Heat the butter in a large saucepan over a low heat until melted, then add the parsnips and apple. Cover and cook for minutes.

Add the stock, sage and cloves and simmer until the parsnip is soft. Remove and discard the cloves, then pour the contents of the saucepan into the bowl of a food processor and process until smooth.

Pour the soup into warmed bowls, add a swirl of cream to each then garnish with parsley and serve immediately.

**SERVES 4**

## INGREDIENTS

3 tbsp vegetable oil

2 onions, chopped

3 garlic cloves, very finely chopped

2 carrots, chopped

2 celery sticks, chopped

900 g/2 lb uncooked beetroot, peeled

4 large tomatoes, peeled, deseeded and chopped

1.2 litres/2 pints vegetable stock (see page 244)

bouquet garni (bay leaf, parsley sprig)

¼ tsp ground cloves

4 whole pink peppercorns

100 ml/3½ fl oz red wine vinegar

pinch of sugar

salt and freshly ground black pepper

snipped fresh chives and soured cream, to garnish

SERVES 4

# Beetroot Soup

Beetroot grows very well in Ireland and is a favourite salad ingredient. If there were a traditional Irish beetroot soup it would probably be this one.

## METHOD

Heat the oil in a large saucepan over a low heat. Add the onion and garlic and cook for 5 minutes, stirring occasionally, until softened but not browned.

Add the carrots, celery and beetroot and cook for 5 minutes, stirring occasionally, then add the tomatoes and cook for a further 2 minutes, stirring.

Add the stock, bouquet garni, cloves and peppercorns and bring to the boil, then reduce the heat and simmer for at least hour, until all the vegetables are very soft.

Remove and discard the bouquet garni, transfer the soup to the bowl of a food processor and process until smooth. Return to the saucepan, stir in the vinegar and sugar with salt and peppe to taste and reheat over a low heat. Do not boil.

Ladle into warmed bowls, garnish with chives and a swirl of soured cream and serve immediately.

## INGREDIENTS

2 tbsp butter

850 ml/1½ pints
fresh vegetable stock
(see page 244)

700 ml/1¼ pints
milk

3 tbsp rolled oats

6 large leeks, cut
into 2.5-cm/1-inch
chunks

salt and freshly
ground black pepper

1 tbsp chopped fresh
parsley, plus extra to
garnish

150 ml/5 fl oz single
cream, to garnish

# Brotchán

## A delicious hearty winter soup that is both economical and filling.

## METHOD

Put the butter, stock and milk into a large saucepan over a medium heat and bring to the boil.

Add the oats, bring back to the boil and cook for 5 minutes, then add the leeks and season to taste with salt and pepper. Cover, reduce the heat and simmer for 30 minutes.

Add the parsley and cook for a further 5 minutes. Transfer to warmed bowls, add a swirl of cream to each, scatter over some parsley and serve immediately.

**SERVES 6**

# Hearty Vegetable Soup

A good vegetable soup can be prepared using whatever vegetables you have to hand. This soup has great texture and substance.

## INGREDIENTS

1 tbsp vegetable oil
25 g/1 oz butter
1 large onion, very finely chopped
1 garlic clove, very finely chopped
4 carrots, thinly sliced
2 celery sticks, thinly sliced
1 potato, diced
1 parsnip, diced
2 small leeks, sliced
850 ml/1½ pints vegetable stock (see page 244)
300 ml/10 fl oz milk
25 g/1 oz cornflour
2 tbsp chopped fresh parsley
salt and freshly ground black pepper

## METHOD

Heat the oil and butter in a large saucepan over a medium heat until the butter is melted. Add the onion, garlic, carrots and celery and cook for 5–10 minutes, stirring occasionally, until softened and just beginning to colour.

Add the potato, parsnip, leeks and stock and bring to the boil, then reduce the heat and simmer for 30 minutes, or until all the vegetables are tender.

Mix a little milk with the cornflour to make a smooth paste, then stir into the soup. Add the remaining milk and bring to the boil, then simmer for 5 minutes. Stir in the parsley, season to taste with salt and pepper and serve immediately in warmed bowls.

SERVES 6

## INGREDIENTS

2 tbsp vegetable oil

1 onion, very finely chopped

4 garlic cloves, very finely chopped

400 g/14 oz Savoy cabbage, finely shredded

4 potatoes, cut into small chunks

1.2 litres/2 pints boiling water

salt and freshly ground black pepper

croûtons (see page 224), to garnish

# Potato & Cabbage Soup Ⓥ

This soup, which combines two tradition Irish ingredients, has a wonderful texture which can only be achieved by using real floury potatoes.

## METHOD

Put the oil into a large saucepan and add the onions and garli Cook over a low heat, stirring occasionally, until softened but not browned.

Add the cabbage and cook for 10 minutes, stirring from time to time to make sure that the cabbage doesn't stick to the saucepan.

Add the potatoes and water, season to taste with salt and pepper, increase the heat and bring to the boil. Reduce the heat and simmer for 20 minutes, or until all the vegetables are cooked through.

Remove from the heat and use a potato masher to purée the soup. Return to the saucepan and reheat, stirring. Do not boil

Ladle into warmed bowls, garnish with croûtons and serve immediately.

**SERVES 4**

## INGREDIENTS

2 garlic bulbs
1 tbsp olive oil
1 tbsp butter
1 small onion, very
finely chopped
2 tbsp plain flour
1 tbsp white wine
vinegar
1 litre/1¾ pints
vegetable stock (see
page 244)
1 litre/1¾ pints
water
2 egg yolks, beaten
salt and freshly
ground black pepper
croûtons (see page
224), to garnish

**SERVES 6**

# Garlic Soup

This unusual soup is enriched with egg
yolks. The strong flavour of the garlic
mellows when it's cooked, so don't be
tempted to reduce the quantity used.

## METHOD

Preheat the oven to 200°C/400°F/Gas Mark 6. Cut the top off each
garlic bulb, place on a baking tray lined with foil and bake in the
preheated oven for 20–30 minutes until the garlic flesh is soft,
then remove from the oven and leave to cool.

Heat the oil and butter in a large saucepan over a low heat until
the butter is melted. Add the onion and cook for 10 minutes,
stirring occasionally, until softened but not browned. Squeeze
the flesh out of the garlic cloves and add to the onion, stirring to
combine.

Add the flour, stirring to make a smooth paste, and cook for 1–
minutes. Increase the heat, add the vinegar, stock and water and
bring to the boil. Reduce the heat and simmer for 10–15 minut

Add a ladleful of the soup to the egg yolks and whisk to combin
then pour into the saucepan and heat over a low heat. Do not
allow to boil or simmer, or the eggs will curdle. Add a little salt
and pepper to taste.

Ladle the soup into warmed bowls, garnish with croûtons and
serve immediately.

## INGREDIENTS

3 tbsp butter

500 g/1 lb 2 oz potatoes, cut into chunks

1 small onion, thinly sliced

1 small leek, thickly sliced

1 litre/1¾ pints vegetable stock (see page 244)

175 g/6 oz fresh young nettle leaves, finely chopped, plus extra whole leaves, to garnish

150 ml/5 fl oz milk

salt and freshly ground black pepper

# Nettle Soup

This traditional spring soup is made with fresh young nettle leaves. As with any young leaf, they require very little cookin

## METHOD

Heat the butter in a large saucepan over a low heat until melted, then add the potatoes, onion and leek and toss to co Add salt and pepper to taste, cover and cook for 10 minutes.

Add the stock, increase the heat and bring to the boil, then reduce the heat and simmer for 10 minutes.

Add the nettle leaves and cook very briefly. Add the milk and stir, then pour into the bowl of a food processor and process until smooth.

Return to the saucepan and heat through, then season to tast and ladle into warmed bowls. Garnish with nettle leaves and serve immediately.

**SERVES 6**

## INGREDIENTS

1 small pumpkin,
about 1.5 kg/3 lb
5 oz

4 tbsp olive oil

2 onions, finely
chopped

3 garlic cloves, finely
chopped

2.5-cm/1-inch piece
fresh ginger, peeled
and chopped

1 tsp ground
coriander

½ tsp ground cumin

pinch of cayenne
pepper

1 litre/1¾ pints
vegetable stock (see
page 244)

salt and freshly
ground black pepper

fresh parsley sprigs,
to garnish

**SERVES 4**

# Pumpkin Soup Ⓥ

Roasting the pumpkin not only intensifie
its flavour, but makes it much easier to
scoop out the flesh.

## METHOD

Preheat the oven to 200°C/400°F/Gas Mark 6. Prick the
pumpkin all over with a skewer, brush with a little oil and ba
in the preheated oven for 45–50 minutes. Remove from the
oven and set aside until cool enough to handle, then split th
pumpkin open and scoop out the flesh, discarding the seeds
Chop the flesh into small chunks.

Heat the remaining oil in a large saucepan over a low heat. A
the onions, garlic and ginger and cook for 5 minutes, then ac
the herbs and spices and cook for a further 2 minutes.

Add the pumpkin flesh and the stock and bring to the boil, t
reduce the heat and simmer for 20–30 minutes.

Transfer the soup to the bowl of a food processor and proce
until smooth. Return to the saucepan, season to taste with sa
and pepper and reheat over a low heat. Do not boil.

Ladle the soup into warmed bowls, garnish with parsley and
serve immediately.

## INGREDIENTS

10 potatoes, peeled
and sliced

5 leeks, trimmed
and thinly sliced

1.5 litres/2½ pints
water

4–6 tbsp single
cream

salt and freshly
ground black pepper

2–3 tbsp chopped
fresh parsley or
chives, to garnish

# Leek & Potato Soup

A delicious winter lunch dish – if you
prefer a lighter soup, replace the cream
with an equal quantity of milk.

## METHOD

Put the potatoes and leeks into a large saucepan of lightly sal
water, bring to the boil and cook for 15–20 minutes, or until
tender.

Remove from the heat and mash the vegetables in the liquid.
Add salt and pepper to taste and return to the heat. Stir in th
cream and warm through over a low heat. Do not boil.

Ladle into warmed bowls, garnish with parsley or chives and
serve immediately.

**SERVES 6**

## INGREDIENTS

2 tbsp olive oil
2 onions, chopped
2 tbsp plain flour
1.2 litres/2 pints
vegetable stock (see
page 244)
salt and freshly
ground black pepper
finely chopped fresh
parsley, to garnish

# Onion Soup Ⓥ

A light, delicious soup that can be
prepared in just over half an hour, using
the most basic ingredients.

## METHOD

Heat the oil in a large saucepan over a low heat. Add the onion
and fry until softened. Add the flour and a little stock and mix
to combine. Add the remaining stock, season to taste with salt
and pepper and cook over a low heat for 30 minutes until
slightly thickened.

Ladle into warmed bowls, garnish with chopped parsley and
serve immediately.

**SERVES 6**

## INGREDIENTS

55 g/2 oz butter

225 g/8 oz potatoes, diced

115 g/4 oz button mushrooms, sliced

1 onion, sliced

450 g/1 lb spinach, chopped

1 litre/1¾ pints vegetable stock (see page 244)

¼ tsp ground cloves

115 g/4 oz rolled oats

salt and freshly ground black pepper

single cream, to garnish

# Spinach & Mushroom Soup

This hearty main course soup is thickene
with oatmeal rather than flour or
cornflour, giving it a satisfying texture.

## METHOD

Heat the butter in a large saucepan over a low heat until
melted. Add the potatoes, mushrooms and onion and fry unti
softened.

Add the spinach, stock and cloves and season to taste with sa
and pepper.

Stir in the oats, bring to the boil, then reduce the heat and
simmer for about 20 minutes. Transfer to a blender and blen
until smooth. Return to the saucepan and reheat. Do not boi

Ladle into warmed bowls, garnish with a swirl of cream and
serve immediately.

**SERVES 4**

## INGREDIENTS

bouquet garni made
from coriander and 1
blade of mace
2 tbsp butter
1 large potato,
peeled and chopped
1 onion, chopped
4 carrots, chopped
3 celery sticks,
chopped
1.7 litres/3 pints
vegetable stock (see
page 244)
55 g/2 oz brown
lentils
30 g/1 oz ground
rice
125 ml/4 fl oz milk
125 ml/4 fl oz single
cream
salt and freshly
ground black pepper
fresh coriander
sprigs, to garnish

# Potato & Vegetable Soup

The mace in this recipe helps to bring ou
the earthy flavours of the root vegetables
lifting this otherwise very simple soup ou
of the ordinary.

## METHOD

Add the mace to the bouquet garni. Melt the butter in a
saucepan, add the vegetables, and toss. Cook gently until the
have absorbed the fat but are not browned.

Add the stock and the lentils, bring to the boil and simmer fo
45 minutes. Remove and discard the bouquet garni, transfer
soup to the bowl of a food processor and process until smoo

Return to the saucepan and thicken with the ground rice.
Season with salt and pepper, then add the milk and cream ar
heat over a low heat. Do not boil.

Serve in warmed bowls, garnished with coriander sprigs.

**SERVES 6**

# HOT & SPICY
Hot & Spicy Soups

## INGREDIENTS

2 tbsp vegetable oil

1 onion, very finely chopped

1 garlic clove, very finely chopped

1 small red chilli, deseeded and very finely chopped

2 tsp finely grated fresh ginger

6 parsnips, diced

1 tsp cumin seeds

½ tsp ground coriander

1 tsp ground turmeric

1.2 litres/2 pints vegetable stock (see page 244)

salt and freshly ground black pepper

natural yogurt and sesame seeds, to garnish

**SERVES 4**

# Curried Parsnip Soup

The sweetness of the parsnips is complemented by the warmth of the spices in this unusual soup. Turmeric giv<br>it a lovely golden colour.

## METHOD

Heat the oil in a large saucepan over a low heat. Add the onio<br>garlic, chilli and ginger and cook for 5 minutes, or until the onion is softened but not browned.

Add the parsnips and cook, stirring occasionally, for 3 minute<br>Add the dried spices and cook for a further 1 minute, stirring constantly to coat the parsnips.

Add the stock, season to taste with salt and pepper and bring<br>the boil. Reduce the heat and simmer for 10–15 minutes unti<br>the parsnips are softened.

Transfer the soup to the bowl of a food processor and proces<br>until smooth, then return it to the saucepan and reheat over<br>low heat. Do not boil.

Ladle the soup into warmed bowls, add a swirl of yogurt to ea<br>portion, sprinkle with sesame seeds and serve immediately.

# Mulligatawny

This spicy soup became fashionable in the 18th century when it was brought back from India by those serving in the British administration there.

## INGREDIENTS

1 tbsp vegetable oil
½ small turnip, diced
1 carrot, diced
2 small onions, diced
450 g/1 lb neck of lamb, trimmed of fat
1.2 litres/2 pints water
1 small apple, diced
1 tsp finely chopped fresh parsley
1 fresh thyme sprig
1 blade of mace
½ tsp cornflour, mixed with 1 tbsp water
1 tsp mild curry powder
salt and freshly ground pepper

## METHOD

Heat the oil in a large saucepan over a low heat. Add the turnip, carrot and onions and fry for 5 minutes, until softened but not browned.

Add the meat and fry, stirring, until browned all over.

Add the water, apple, parsley, thyme, mace and cornflour, stirring constantly. Increase the heat and bring to the boil, then add the curry powder. Reduce the heat and simmer for 3 hours.

Remove the lamb with a slotted spoon, then take the meat off the bones, discarding the bones, and chop into chunks. Return the meat to the soup, season to taste with salt and pepper.

Ladle into warmed bowls and serve immediately.

SERVES 4

## INGREDIENTS

2 large aubergines

2 tbsp olive oil, plus extra for brushing

5 spring onions, very finely chopped

2 garlic cloves, very finely chopped

1 fresh green chilli, very finely chopped

115 g/4 oz small button mushrooms

1 tsp ground cumin

1 tsp ground coriander

1 tsp ground turmeric

salt

400 g/14 oz canned chopped tomatoes

1 tbsp chopped fresh coriander

450 ml/16 fl oz vegetable stock (see page 244)

fresh coriander sprigs, to garnish

SERVES 4

# Roasted Aubergine Soup

Roasting the aubergines gives them a lovely earthy flavour that works well in this coarse-textured soup.

## METHOD

Preheat the oven to 200°C/400°F/Gas Mark 6. Brush the aubergines with oil, prick them all over with a fork and roast in the preheated oven for 35 minutes.

Meanwhile, heat the oil in a large saucepan over a low heat, add the onions, garlic, chilli and mushrooms and fry, stirring occasionally, for 5 minutes. Add the herbs and spices and a little salt to taste and fry for a further 3 minutes.

Add the tomatoes, increase the heat and bring to the boil, then reduce the heat and simmer for 5 minutes.

When the aubergines are cool enough to handle, cut them in half lengthwise and scoop out the flesh into a bowl. Mash with a fork until you have a coarse texture.

Add the aubergine flesh to the saucepan with the fresh coriander, then add the stock and bring to the boil. Reduce the heat and simmer for 5 minutes.

Ladle into warmed bowls, garnish with coriander sprigs and serve immediately.

## INGREDIENTS

1 tbsp vegetable oil

500 g/1 lb 2 oz
carrots, thinly sliced

1 large onion, finely
chopped

1 Bramley apple,
peeled and roughly
chopped

1 tbsp mild curry
powder

700 ml/1¼ pints
vegetable stock (see
page 244)

salt and freshly
ground black pepper

croûtons (see page
224) and fresh
coriander sprigs, to
garnish

# Curried Carrot & Apple Soup Ⓥ

An extremely simple and quick soup that
has a sweet and spicy hit.

## METHOD

Heat the oil in a large saucepan over a low heat, add the carrot,
onion and apple, then stir in the curry powder until all the
ingredients are coated. Cover and cook for 15 minutes.

Transfer the contents of the saucepan to the bowl of a food
processor, add half the stock and process until smooth.

Return to the saucepan, add the remaining stock and bring to
the boil. Season to taste with salt and pepper, and ladle into
warmed bowls. Garnish with croûtons and coriander and serve
immediately.

SERVES 4

## INGREDIENTS

250 g/9 oz
cauliflower florets

250 g/9 oz broccoli
florets

700 ml/1¼ pints
milk

1 tbsp garam masala

salt and freshly
ground black pepper

rocket leaves, to
garnish

# Curried Cauliflower & Broccoli Soup

With only four ingredients, this soup is very quick to prepare. If you like, substitute some of the florets with an equal weight of chopped cauliflower and broccoli stalks.

## METHOD

Put the cauliflower and broccoli into a large saucepan, add the milk and garam masala and season to taste with salt and pepper

Bring to the boil over a medium heat, then reduce the heat and simmer for 20 minutes, or until the vegetables are tender.

Transfer the soup to the bowl of a food processor and process until smooth, then return to the saucepan and reheat over a low heat. Do not boil.

Ladle the soup into warmed bowls, garnish with rocket and serve immediately.

**SERVES 4**

## INGREDIENTS

2 tbsp vegetable oil
1 onion, chopped
1 parsnip, chopped
1 turnip, chopped
1 potato, chopped
3 carrots, chopped
2.5-cm/1-inch piece
fresh ginger, grated
1.5 litres/2¾ pints
vegetable stock (see
page 244)
300 ml/10 fl oz milk
2 tbsp chopped
fresh dill
salt and freshly
ground black pepper
fresh dill sprigs, to
garnish

# Vegetable Soup with Dill & Ginger

Ginger is the perfect complement to root vegetables in this unusual winter soup.

## METHOD

Put the oil into a large saucepan with the vegetables and ginger and cook over a low heat for 15 minutes, stirring occasionally prevent sticking.

Add the stock, increase the heat and bring to the boil. Season to taste with salt and pepper, reduce the heat and simmer for 15–20 minutes.

Transfer the soup to the bowl of a food processor and process until smooth. Return to the saucepan, add the milk and reheat over a low heat. Do not boil.

Stir in the chopped dill, ladle into warmed bowls, garnish with dill sprigs and serve immediately.

SERVES 6

## INGREDIENTS

2 tbsp olive oil
1 onion, very finely chopped
1 tsp ground cumin
1 tsp garam masala
¼ tsp turmeric
1 tsp chopped fresh coriander
2.5-cm/1-inch piece fresh ginger, finely grated
250 g/9 oz tomatoes, peeled and roughly chopped
1 green chilli, very finely chopped
400 g/14 oz canned chickpeas, rinsed and drained
400 ml/14 fl oz canned coconut milk
salt and freshly ground black pepper
fresh coriander sprigs, to garnish

# Spicy Chickpea & Tomato Soup Ⓥ

This chunky, spicy soup is a perfect winter warmer and can be prepared in 1⁵ minutes.

## METHOD

Put the oil into a large saucepan with the onion, cumin, garam masala, turmeric, coriander and ginger and cook over a low heat until the onion is softened but not browned.

Add the tomatoes, chilli and chickpeas and cook, stirring, for minutes.

Add the coconut milk, season to taste with salt and pepper an heat through. Do not boil.

Ladle into warmed bowls, garnish with coriander and serve immediately.

**SERVES 4**

## INGREDIENTS

1 tbsp vegetable oil

1 onion, very finely chopped

300 g/10½ oz carrots, thinly sliced

350 g/12 oz sweet potatoes, diced

1 tsp ground coriander

1 tsp ground cumin

1 tsp chilli powder

850 ml/1½ pints vegetable stock (see page 244)

salt and freshly ground black pepper

paprika and snipped fresh chives, to garnish

# Spicy Sweet Potato & Carrot Soup Ⓥ

The sweetness of the potatoes and carrot is complemented by the spices in this colourful winter soup.

## METHOD

Heat the oil in a large saucepan over a low heat. Add the onio carrots and sweet potatoes and cook for 5 minutes, stirring occasionally, until the carrots and sweet potatoes are tender. Add the ground coriander, cumin and chilli powder and cook for 1 minute, stirring.

Add the stock, increase the heat and bring to the boil, then reduce the heat, cover and cook for 35 minutes.

Transfer the soup to the bowl of a food processor and proces until smooth. Season to taste with salt and pepper, return to saucepan and reheat over a low heat. Do not boil.

Ladle into warmed bowls, garnish with paprika and chives an serve immediately.

**SERVES 4**

## INGREDIENTS

4 tbsp olive oil

1 onion, very finely chopped

1 green chilli, deseeded and very finely chopped

3 garlic cloves, very finely chopped

900 g/2 lb courgettes, trimmed and chopped

250 g/9 oz day-old bread, cubed

700 ml/1¼ pints vegetable stock (see page 244)

250 ml/9 fl oz water

3 tbsp chopped fresh mint leaves

2 tsp lemon juice

salt and freshly ground black pepper

fresh mint sprigs, to garnish

# Fresh & Spicy Courgette Soup Ⓥ

This is a great recipe if you have a glut of courgettes and some day-old bread. It can be served hot or cold.

## METHOD

Heat the oil in a large saucepan over a low heat. Add the onion and chilli and cook for 5 minutes until the onion is softened b not browned. Add the garlic and courgettes and cook, stirring frequently, for 4 minutes. Season to taste with salt.

Add the bread, stock and water, increase the heat and bring to simmer, then reduce the heat and simmer for 20 minutes.

Transfer to the bowl of a food processor, add the mint and process until smooth. Return to the saucepan, add the lemon juice and salt and pepper to taste and heat through. Do not boil.

Ladle into warmed bowls, garnish with mint sprigs and serve immediately, or chill in the refrigerator for at least 2 hours before serving.

**SERVES 4-6**

## INGREDIENTS

2 tbsp sunflower oil
25 g/1 oz butter
1 large onion, finely chopped
2 large potatoes, diced
500 ml/18 fl oz milk
500 ml/18 fl oz hot vegetable stock (see page 244)
1 tsp whole black peppercorns
pinch of salt
freshly ground black pepper, to garnish

# Potato Soup with Black Pepper

Black pepper is often treated as a condiment rather than a fiery spice in its own right. Using whole black peppercorn increases the level of heat.

## METHOD

Heat the oil and butter in a large saucepan over a medium heat until the butter is melted. Add the onion and cook for 5 minutes until the onion is softened but not browned.

Add the potatoes and cook for 10–15 minutes, then add the milk, stock and peppercorns and bring to the boil. Reduce the heat and simmer for 15–20 minutes until the potatoes are tender. Add the salt.

Transfer to the bowl of a food processor and process until smooth, making sure that none of the peppercorns remain whole.

Ladle the soup into warmed bowls, garnish with pepper and serve immediately.

**SERVES 4**

## INGREDIENTS

3 red peppers, halved and deseeded

1 onion, unpeeled and halved

4 garlic cloves, unpeeled

2 tbsp olive oil

25 g/1 oz butter

2 celery sticks, roughly chopped

450 ml/16 fl oz vegetable stock (see page 244)

3 tbsp sun-dried tomato purée

1 tsp dried chilli flakes

500 g/1 lb 2 oz canned chopped tomatoes

salt and freshly ground black pepper

double cream and fresh rosemary sprigs, to garnish

# Roasted Red Pepper & Sun-drie Tomato Soup

Follow this recipe for a spicy twist on th simple traditional tomato soup.

## METHOD

Preheat the oven to 200°C/400°F/Gas Mark 6. Place the pepp onion halves (cut side down) and garlic cloves on a baking tray and drizzle with the oil. Bake in the preheated oven for minutes or until the vegetables are tender.

Meanwhile, put the butter into a large saucepan over a medi heat and heat until melted. Add the celery and sauté for 4–5 minutes. Add the stock, tomato purée and chilli flakes and m well to combine. Remove from the heat.

Peel the onion and the garlic cloves, then chop them and ad to the pan with the canned tomatoes. Heat over a low–medi heat until just simmering, then blend until smooth. Season t taste with salt and pepper.

Divide the soup among four warmed bowls, garnish with a s of cream and some rosemary and serve immediately.

**SERVES 4**

# FISH & SEAFOOD
Fish & Seafood Soups

## INGREDIENTS

2 tbsp olive oil

2 large leeks, green and white parts separated, sliced

1 tsp crushed coriander seeds

¼ tsp dried red chilli flakes

300 g/10½ oz potatoes, thickly sliced

400 g/14 oz canned chopped tomatoes

600 ml/1 pint fish stock (see page 248)

150 ml/5 fl oz dry white wine

1 bay leaf

pinch of saffron threads

450 g/1 lb cod or haddock fillets, cut into chunks

250 g/9 oz peeled raw prawns

450 g/1 lb small squid, cleaned and sliced

3 tbsp chopped fresh parsley

salt and freshly ground black pepper

**SERVES 4**

# Seafood Soup with Leeks & Tomatoes

A delicious main course soup with more than a hint of the Mediterranean. You could use any white fish and combination of seafood.

## METHOD

Heat the oil in a large heavy-based saucepan over a low heat, then add the green leek slices, coriander seeds and chilli flakes. Cook, stirring occasionally, for 5 minutes, or until the leeks are softened but not browned.

Add the potatoes, tomatoes, stock, wine, bay leaf and saffron and stir to combine. Increase the heat and bring to the boil, then reduce the heat and simmer for 20 minutes until the potatoes are tender. Season to taste with salt and pepper.

Add the fish to the soup and cook for 5 minutes. Add the prawns and cook for a further 1 minute. Add the squid and the white leek slices and cook, stirring occasionally, for a further 2 minutes.

Stir in the parsley, ladle into warmed bowls and serve immediately.

## INGREDIENTS

55 g/2 oz butter
1 large onion, finely chopped
115 g/4 oz smoked bacon lardons
4 celery sticks, diced
2 potatoes, diced
400 g/14 oz canned chopped tomatoes, strained to remove the seeds
450 ml/16 fl oz fish stock (see page 248)
450 g/1 lb white fish fillets
225 g/8 oz mixed cooked shellfish
200 ml/7 fl oz milk
100 ml/3½ fl oz single cream
salt and freshly ground black pepper
chopped fresh parsley, to garnish

# Classic Fish Chowder

This indulgent soup is incredibly easy to prepare. The key to success is a really good fish stock.

## METHOD

Heat the butter in a large saucepan over a low heat until melted. Add the onion, lardons, celery and potatoes and stir t coat with the butter. Cover and cook for 5–10 minutes, until the vegetables are beginning to soften.

Add the tomatoes and stock, increase the heat to medium and bring to the boil, then reduce the heat and simmer until the potatoes are tender.

Add the fish and shellfish to the soup, then add the milk and cream and bring to the boil. Reduce the heat and simmer for 3–4 minutes, or until the fish is cooked through. Add salt and pepper to taste.

Ladle into warmed bowls, garnish with parsley and serve immediately.

**SERVES 6**

## INGREDIENTS

25 g/1 oz butter
1 onion, finely chopped
1 garlic clove, finely chopped
1 fennel bulb, trimmed and finely chopped
1 leek, finely chopped
25 g/1 oz plain flour
1.7 litres/3 pints fish stock (see page 248)
2 potatoes, diced
450 g/1 lb boneless, skinless salmon, cut into bite-sized pieces
200 ml/7 fl oz milk
100 ml/3 fl oz double cream
2 tbsp chopped fresh dill
salt and freshly ground black pepper
chopped fresh flatleaf parsley, to garnish

**SERVES 4**

# Salmon Chowder

The sweetness of fennel is a wonderful complement to fish and is enhanced here with the addition of dill, often referred to as the 'fish herb'.

## METHOD

Heat the butter in a large saucepan over a low heat until melted. Add the onion, garlic, fennel and leek, increase the he to medium and cook, stirring occasionally, for 5–10 minutes until the vegetables are softened.

Add the flour and stir. Reduce the heat to low and cook for 2– minutes, stirring occasionally, then add the stock and potatoe and season to taste with salt and pepper. Bring to the boil over a medium heat, then reduce the heat and simmer for 3–! minutes.

Add the salmon and simmer for a further 3–5 minutes until it is just cooked. Add the milk, cream and dill and cook until the soup is just warmed through. Do not boil.

Ladle into warmed bowls, garnish with chopped parsley and serve immediately.

## INGREDIENTS

400 g/14 oz sweet
potatoes, peeled and
cubed

225 g/8 oz peeled
and deseeded
butternut squash,
cubed

55 g/2 oz butter

1 onion, finely
chopped

450 g/1 lb skinless
smoked haddock
fillets

600 ml/1 pint milk

4 tbsp double cream

salt and freshly
ground black pepper

**SERVES 6**

# Smoked Haddock Chowder

This lovely soup gets its vibrant colour
from smoked haddock, butternut squash
and sweet potatoes.

## METHOD

Bring two separate saucepans of lightly salted water to the boil, a
the sweet potatoes to one and the squash to the other, bring back
to the boil and cook for 15 minutes or until just tender. Drain and
set aside.

Heat half the butter in a large heavy-based saucepan over a low he
until melted. Add the onion and cook for 5 minutes until softene
but not browned.

Add the haddock to the saucepan with enough water to cover,
increase the heat and bring to the boil, then reduce the heat and
simmer for 10 minutes, or until the fish is cooked. Remove from
the water with a slotted spoon and set aside to cool. Reserve the
cooking liquid.

Use a fork to roughly flake the fish, discarding any bones.

Mash the sweet potatoes with the remaining butter and salt and
pepper to taste.

Strain the reserved cooking liquid, return it to the saucepan and
whisk in the sweet potato mash. Add the milk, stirring well and
bring to the boil, then reduce the heat and simmer for 2–3 minut

Add the squash, haddock and cream and heat through. Do not bo
Ladle into warmed bowls and serve immediately.

## INGREDIENTS

600 ml/1 pint milk

100 ml/3½ fl oz double cream

450 g/1 lb skinned and boned haddock fillet

2 tbsp olive oil

1 small onion, finely sliced

1 garlic clove, finely chopped

300 g/10½ oz potatoes, cubed

300 g/10½ oz baby broad beans, shelled

175 g/6 oz baby spinach leaves

salt and freshly ground black pepper

**SERVES 4**

# Haddock, Spinach & Broad Bean Soup

A fresh-tasting soup that makes the most of young spring vegetables. You could use any firm white fish if haddock is unavailable.

## METHOD

Put the milk into a large saucepan with the cream and bring to the boil over a medium heat. Add the fish and bring back to the boil, then reduce the heat and simmer for 6 minutes, or until just cooked. Remove the fish from the liquid using a slotted spoon. Reserve the cooking liquid.

Use a fork to flake the fish roughly, discarding any bones, then set aside until needed.

Heat the oil in a large saucepan, then add the onion and garlic and cook for 5 minutes, or until softened but not browned. Add the potatoes, then stir in the reserved cooking liquid and bring to the boil. Reduce the heat and simmer for 10 minutes, then add the beans and cook for a further 5 minutes until the potatoes and beans are tender.

Add the fish and heat through over a low heat. Do not boil. Add the spinach, stirring until just wilted, then season to taste with salt and pepper.

Ladle the soup into warmed bowls and serve immediately.

## INGREDIENTS

350 g/12 oz Finnan
haddock fillet

1 onion, finely
chopped

bouquet garni
(thyme sprigs,
parsley sprigs, fennel
sprigs)

500 g/1 lb 2 oz
potatoes, cubed

55 g/2 oz butter

600 ml/1 pint milk

fish stock (see page
248)

salt and freshly
ground black pepper

chopped fresh
flatleaf parsley, to
garnish

# Cullen Skink

This classic Scottish soup uses cold-
smoked Finnan haddock, which is more
lightly smoked than the regular variety.

## METHOD

Put the fish, onion and bouquet garni into a large saucepan
and add enough water to cover completely. Bring to the boil,
skimming off any scum that rises to the surface, then reduce th
heat and simmer for 10 minutes, or until the fish is flaking.

Remove the fish from the saucepan with a slotted spoon, set
aside to cool slightly, then flake it roughly, removing the bones
and skin. Add the bones and skin to the saucepan and simmer
for 30 minutes.

Strain the cooking liquid and return to the saucepan, then add
the potatoes and cook for 10–15 minutes until tender. Remove
from the liquid with a slotted spoon, then mash with the butte

Add the milk to the stock and bring to the boil, then whisk in
the mashed potato. Add the fish and heat through. Do not boil

Season to taste with salt and pepper, then ladle into warmed
bowls, garnish with parsley and serve immediately.

SERVES 6

## INGREDIENTS

3 tbsp olive oil

1 large onion, very finely chopped

4 garlic cloves, very finely chopped

2 leeks, finely sliced

400 g/14 oz canned chopped tomatoes

3 litres/5¼ pints hot fish stock (see page 248)

bouquet garni (thyme sprigs, bay leaves, fennel sprigs)

2.5 kg/5 lb 8 oz mixed firm white fish, such as monkfish, cod and haddock, cut into large pieces

4 potatoes, thickly sliced

salt and freshly ground black pepper

chopped fresh parsley, to garnish

**SERVES 4–6**

# Mediterranean Fish Soup

This hearty soup originates in southern France, where there are as many variations as there are varieties of fish.

## METHOD

Heat the oil in a large saucepan over a medium heat, then add the onion, garlic, leeks and tomatoes. Stir to combine, then cook for 10 minutes, or until the onions and leeks are softened. Stir in the stock, add the bouquet garni and bring to the boil, then reduce the heat and add the fish and potatoes.

Simmer for about 8 minutes, removing the fish when it is cooked through, then continue to cook until the potatoes are tender. Season to taste with salt and pepper. Return the fish to the soup and heat through. Do not boil.

To serve, remove the fish and potatoes with a slotted spoon and divide among four warmed bowls. Strain the soup and ladle it into the bowls. Garnish with parsley and serve immediately.

## INGREDIENTS

700 ml/1¼ pints dry white wine

1 carrot, thinly sliced

3 celery sticks

3 kg/6 lb 8 oz mussels, scrubbed and debearded

3 onions, sliced

2 bay leaves

8 pink peppercorns

2 leeks, thinly sliced

85 g/3 oz cornflour

200 ml/7 fl oz single cream

salt and freshly ground black pepper

snipped fresh chives and fresh thyme sprigs, to garnish

**SERVES 4**

# Mussel Soup

This recipe is based on the classic recipe for moules marinières, but is a bit more substantial.

## METHOD

Put the wine into a large saucepan with an equal quantity of water, add the carrot and celery and season well with salt and pepper. Bring to the boil, then reduce the heat and simmer for 50 minutes.

Discard any mussels with broken shells or any that do not open when tapped. Put them into a saucepan with the onions, bay leaves, peppercorns and a little water and cook over a high heat, shaking the saucepan from time to time, for 5 minutes, until the mussel shells have opened.

Remove the mussels with a slotted spoon, reserving the cooking liquid. Discard any mussels that remain closed and remove three-quarters of the remainder from their shells.

Strain 500 ml/18 fl oz of the cooking liquid through a muslin-lined sieve and add to the wine mixture. Add the leeks and cook for 2 minutes. Mix the cornflour with a little soup, then stir into the soup and bring to the boil, stirring constantly.

Remove from the heat and stir in the cream and mussels. Divide among warmed bowls, making sure that there are some unshelled mussels in each portion, garnish with chives and thyme and serve immediately.

## INGREDIENTS

175 g/6 oz skinned monkfish fillet, cut into large chunks

1 small onion, finely chopped

1 large sweet potato, diced

1 carrot, chopped

½ tsp dried oregano

1.3 litres/2¼ pints fish stock (see page 248)

100 ml/3½ fl oz single cream

salt and freshly ground black pepper

fresh parsley sprigs, to garnish

# Monkfish & Sweet Potato Soup

Monkfish has a very distinctive flavour, which is complemented here by the oregano and sweet potato.

## METHOD

Put the fish into a large saucepan with the vegetables, oregano and half the stock. Bring to the boil, then reduce the heat and simmer for 10–15 minutes until the sweet potato is tender.

Leave to cool, then transfer to the bowl of a food processor and process until smooth. Return to the saucepan, stir in the remaining stock and bring to the boil. Reduce the heat and st in the cream. Do not boil. Add salt and pepper to taste.

Ladle into warmed bowls, garnish with parsley and serve immediately.

**SERVES 4**

## INGREDIENTS

200 g/7 oz canned sweetcorn
600 ml/1 pint milk
25 g/1 oz butter
1 small leek, finely sliced
55 g/2 oz smoked bacon lardons
1 garlic clove, finely chopped
1 celery stick, finely chopped
1 potato, diced
1 tbsp cornflour
300 ml/10 fl oz fish stock (see page 248)
4 scallops, corals removed and reserved
125 g/4½ oz cooked mussels
150 ml/5 fl oz single cream
salt and freshly ground black pepper

**SERVES 6**

# Scallop, Mussel & Sweetcorn Chowder

This main course soup is full of wonderf
flavour, with the bacon perfectly
complementing the scallops and the corr
adding sweetness and texture.

## METHOD

Put half the sweetcorn into the bowl of a food processor with
little milk and process until smooth.

Heat the butter in a large saucepan over a low heat until
melted, then add the leek, lardons and garlic and fry, stirring
occasionally, for 5 minutes, or until the leek is softened but
not browned. Add the celery and potato, cover and cook for a
further 3–4 minutes, stirring from time to time.

Mix the cornflour with a little stock and stir into the saucepan
then add the sweetcorn and milk mixture and the remaining
stock, milk and sweetcorn kernels. Season to taste with salt a
pepper.

Bring to the boil over a medium heat, then reduce the heat ar
simmer for 15 minutes, or until all the vegetables are tender.

Slice the scallops, stir into the soup and cook for 3 minutes.
Add the reserved corals and the mussels and heat through, th
stir in the cream. do not boil.

Ladle into warmed bowls and serve immediately.

# Smoked Trout & Potato Soup

## INGREDIENTS

1 knob of butter

1 small onion, chopped

1 celery stick, chopped

1 small red pepper, sliced

2 potatoes, chopped

1 litre/1¾ pints fish stock (see page 248)

2 fresh dill sprigs

1 smoked trout fillet

4 tsp crème fraîche

salt and freshly ground black pepper

olive oil and fresh rosemary sprigs, to garnish

A delicate and creamy fish soup that makes the most of a small amount of smoked fish. You can use smoked salmon instead of trout. Because it is smoked, the fish does not need cooking.

## METHOD

Heat the butter in a large saucepan over a low heat until melted, then add the onion, celery, red pepper and salt to taste. Cook, stirring occasionally, until the onions are translucent and the peppers are softened.

Add the potatoes and stir, then add the stock, dill and a little pepper. Increase the heat and bring to the boil, then reduce the heat and simmer until the potatoes are cooked.

Transfer the soup to the bowl of a food processor and process until smooth. Return to the saucepan and reheat until warmed through. Break the fish into bite-sized pieces and add to the soup. Stir in the crème fraîche.

Serve in warmed bowls, garnished with a few drops of oil and some rosemary..

**SERVES 4**

# PASTA, RICE & NOODLES

Soups with Pasta, Rice & Noodles

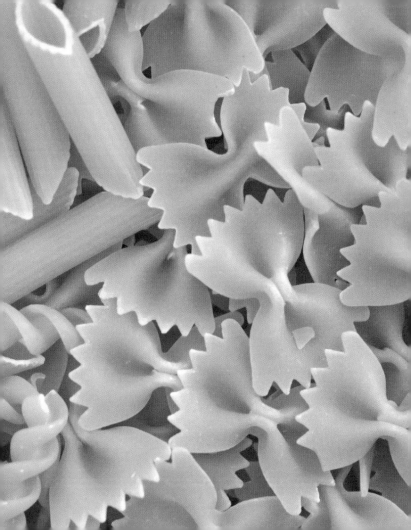

## INGREDIENTS

1 whole chicken,
about 2 kg/4 lb 8 oz

1 large onion, halved

2 large carrots,
roughly chopped

6 celery sticks,
roughly chopped

1 bay leaf

175 g/6 oz
vermicelli pasta

3 tbsp chopped fresh
flatleaf parsley, plus
extra to garnish

salt and freshly
ground black pepper

# Chicken Noodle Soup

This classic clear soup has long been regarded as a fail-safe cure for winter colds. The basic soup is a really good broth – the unused chicken meat can be used in sandwiches or pies.

## METHOD

Put the chicken into a large saucepan with the vegetables and bay leaf and add enough cold water to cover. Bring to the boil over a medium heat, skimming off any scum that appears on surface. Season to taste with salt and pepper, then reduce the heat and simmer for 2 hours.

Remove the chicken, strip the flesh off the carcass and set aside for use in another dish. Return the bones to the saucepan and simmer for a further 1 hour.

Strain the soup into a bowl, then leave to cool. Chill overnight then remove the fat layer that will have formed on top of the liquid (the liquid will have taken on a jelly-like consistency).

Reheat the soup in a large saucepan (the jelly will liquefy) without bringing it to the boil. Add the pasta and parsley and simmer for 6–8 minutes until the pasta is cooked.

Ladle into warmed bowls and serve immediately, garnished with parsley.

**SERVES 6**

## INGREDIENTS

4 tbsp olive oil
1 onion, finely chopped
1 garlic clove, very finely chopped
1 carrot, diced
1 celery stick, diced
1 tsp chopped fresh parsley, plus extra to garnish
1.5 litres/2¾ pints vegetable stock
15 g/½ oz dried porcini mushrooms, rehydrated and finely chopped
85 g/3 oz canned Puy lentils
150 g/5½ oz canned red kidney beans, rinsed and drained
150 g/5½ oz canned cannellini beans, rinsed and drained
150 g/5½ oz canned chickpeas, rinsed and drained
115 g/4 oz dried penne
salt and freshly ground black pepper
freshly grated Parmesan cheese, to serve

**SERVES 6**

# Mixed Pulse & Pasta Soup

Pulses are a popular ingredient in Italy, where there are many variations of this main course soup. The dried mushroom add subtle flavour.

## METHOD

Heat the oil in a large saucepan over a low heat. Add the onio garlic, carrot, celery and parsley and cook, stirring constantly for 5 minutes, or until the vegetables are softened.

Add the stock and the mushrooms and bring to the boil, then add all the pulses and season to taste with salt and pepper. Reduce the heat and simmer for 20 minutes.

Add the pasta and bring back to the boil, stirring occasionally Reduce the heat and simmer for 7–8 minutes, or according t the packet instructions, until the pasta is tender but still firm the bite.

Ladle into warmed bowls, garnish with parsley and serve immediately with some Parmesan cheese on the side.

## INGREDIENTS

4 tbsp olive oil

2 onions, finely
chopped

1.5 litres/2¾ pints
chicken stock (see
page 246)

900 g/2 lb small
courgettes, grated

115 g/4 oz dried
pasta

juice of ½ lemon

1 tbsp chopped fresh
oregano, or 1 tsp
dried oregano

salt and freshly
ground black pepper

soured cream, to
garnish

# Courgette Soup with Pasta

A lovely summer soup, cooked with
pasta. Young courgettes give a fresh
flavour to this soup.

## METHOD

Heat the oil in a large saucepan over a low heat. Add the oni
and cook for 10 minutes, or until softened but not browned.

Add the stock and bring to the boil, then add the courgettes
and pasta. Reduce the heat and simmer for 10–15 minutes, c
until the pasta is tender but still firm to the bite.

Add the lemon juice and salt and pepper to taste, then stir in
the oregano.

Ladle into warmed bowls, garnish with soured cream and se
immediately.

**SERVES 6**

## INGREDIENTS

450 g/1 lb ripe plum tomatoes, halved lengthways

1 large red pepper, halved lengthways and deseeded

1 red onion, quartered

2 unpeeled garlic cloves

1 tbsp olive oil

1.2 litres/2 pints vegetable stock (see page 244)

85 g/3 oz soup pasta

salt and freshly ground black pepper

torn fresh basil leaves, to garnish

# Roasted Tomato & Red Pepper Soup with Pasta Ⓥ

The roasted vegetables give an intense flavour to this soup.

## METHOD

Preheat the oven to 190°C/375°F/Gas Mark 5. Spread the vegetables in a single layer in a roasting tin and drizzle with t oil. Roast in the preheated oven for 30–40 minutes until soft and lightly charred, turning halfway through cooking.

Transfer the vegetables to the bowl of a food processor, add quarter of the stock and process until smooth. Press through sieve into a large saucepan. Add the remaining stock and brin to the boil.

Add the pasta and simmer for 7–8 minutes, or according to t packet instructions, stirring occasionally, until tender but stil firm to the bite. Season to taste with salt and pepper.

Ladle into warmed bowls, garnish with basil and serve immediately.

**SERVES 4**

## INGREDIENTS

3 tbsp olive oil

25 g/1 oz butter

1 onion, finely chopped

2 garlic cloves, very finely chopped

2 celery sticks, finely chopped

400 g/14 oz canned brown lentils

3–4 small tomatoes

1.7 litres/3 pints vegetable stock (see page 244)

1 tsp fresh oregano leaves

½ tsp fresh thyme leaves

small handful fresh basil leaves, torn

100 g/3½ oz dried macaroni

salt and freshly ground black pepper

fresh flatleaf parsley sprigs, to garnish

**SERVES 6**

# Lentil Soup with Macaroni

Lentils and macaroni are staples in every Irish storecupboard and are delicious combined in this substantial winter soup

## METHOD

Heat the oil and butter in a large saucepan over a low heat until the butter is melted. Add the onion, garlic and celery an cook, stirring occasionally, for 5 minutes until softened but n browned.

Add the lentils, tomatoes, stock and herbs and season to taste with salt and pepper. Increase the heat and bring to the boil, stirring constantly, then reduce the heat and simmer for 25 minutes, stirring from time to time.

Add the macaroni, increase the heat and bring back to the bo then reduce the heat and cook for 8–10 minutes, or accordin to the packet instructions, until tender but still firm to the bi

Ladle into warmed bowls, garnish with parsley and serve immediately.

## INGREDIENTS

700 g/1 lb 9 oz
baby spinach leaves,
washed and drained

3 tbsp olive oil

1 onion, very finely
chopped

2 garlic cloves, very
finely chopped

¼ tsp dried red chilli
flakes

225 g/8 oz Arborio
or carnaroli rice

1.2 litres/2 pints
chicken stock (see
page 246)

salt and freshly
ground black pepper

freshly grated
Parmesan cheese,
to serve

# Spinach Soup with Rice

This soup is tastiest when prepared with baby spinach leaves, cooked until they ar barely wilted. Don't add too much salt, a spinach is naturally salty.

## METHOD

Put the spinach into a large saucepan with just the water clinging to its leaves and heat over a very low heat until just wilted. Drain, reserving the cooking liquid, and chop very fin with a knife.

Heat the oil in a large saucepan over a low heat, then add the onion, garlic and chilli flakes and cook for 5 minutes, or unti the onion and garlic are softened but not browned. Add the r and stir until well coated with the oil.

Add the stock and the reserved spinach cooking liquid, increa the heat and bring to the boil. Reduce the heat and simmer fe 10 minutes, stirring occasionally.

Add the spinach, season to taste with salt and pepper and co for a further 5 minutes, or until the rice is tender.

Serve in warmed bowls, with Parmesan cheese on the side.

**SERVES 6**

## INGREDIENTS

1 tbsp vegetable oil
25 g/1 oz butter
6 green cardamom pods
2 small skinless, boneless chicken breasts
2 leeks, thinly sliced
350 g/12 oz pumpkin flesh
850 ml/1½ pints chicken stock (see page 246)
115 g/4 oz basmati rice
350 ml/12 fl oz milk
salt and freshly ground pepper
coarsely grated orange zest, to garnish

**SERVES 4**

# Chicken & Pumpkin Soup with Rice

Cardamom adds an unusual flavour to this soup – it's quite an earthy spice with a slightly sweet finish.

## METHOD

Heat the oil and butter in a large saucepan over a low heat until the butter is melted. Add the cardamom and fry for 3 minutes, until the pods have swelled slightly. Add the chicken, leeks and pumpkin, increase the heat to medium and cook, turning the chicken once, for 5 minutes.

Add two-thirds of the stock and bring to the boil, then reduce the heat and simmer for 15 minutes until the pumpkin is softened and the chicken is cooked through.

Add the remaining stock and the rice, increase the heat and bring to the boil, then reduce the heat and simmer for 10 minutes, or until the rice is tender. Season to taste with salt and pepper.

Remove the chicken and cardamom from the soup, discarding cardamom pods. Slice the chicken into thin strips and set aside.

Pour the soup into the bowl of a food processor and process until the texture is still quite coarse. Return to the saucepan and add the milk and chicken. Reheat until just simmering. Do not boil.

Ladle into warmed bowls, garnish with orange zest and serve immediately.

## INGREDIENTS

5 tbsp olive oil

1 onion, very finely chopped

1 garlic clove, very finely chopped

450 g/1 lb shelled broad beans, blanched and peeled

2 plum tomatoes, peeled and chopped

200 g/7 oz Arborio or carnaroli rice

1 litre/1¾ pints vegetable stock (see page 244)

salt and freshly ground black pepper

# Broad Bean Soup with Rice Ⓥ

This thick soup is a good way to use up a summer glut of broad beans – you don't need tender baby broad beans for this recipe.

## METHOD

Heat the oil in a large saucepan over a low heat. Add the onion and garlic and cook for 5 minutes, or until softened but not browned.

Add the beans, increase the heat and cook for 5–6 minutes, stirring to coat them in the oil. Add the tomatoes, season to taste with salt and pepper and cook, stirring, for a further 5 minutes.

Add the rice and cook for 5 minutes, then gradually add the stock. Cook for a further 10–15 minutes, stirring occasionally, until the rice is tender.

Transfer to warmed bowls and serve immediately.

**SERVES 4**

## INGREDIENTS

115 g/4 oz small pasta shapes

2 tbsp olive oil

5 spring onions, finely chopped

350 g/12 oz shelled fresh peas or frozen peas

1.2 litres/2 pints ham stock (see page 250)

225 g/8 oz cooked ham, diced

4 tbsp double cream

salt and freshly ground black pepper

chopped fresh parsley, to garnish

# Ham & Pea Soup with Pasta

## The classic pea and ham soup gets an Italian twist with the addition of pasta.

### METHOD

Bring a small saucepan of lightly salted water to the boil, add the pasta and cook for 6–8 minutes, or according to the pack instructions, until tender but still firm to the bite. Drain and s aside until needed.

Heat the oil in a heavy saucepan over a low heat. Add the spri onions and cook, stirring, for 5 minutes until softened but no browned. Add the peas and stock, increase the heat and bring to the boil, then reduce the heat and simmer for 5 minutes.

Transfer the soup to the bowl of a food processor and proces until smooth, then return to the saucepan, add the ham and pasta and heat through. Season to taste with salt and pepper and stir in the cream.

Ladle into warmed soup bowls, garnish with parsley and serv immediately.

**SERVES 4**

## INGREDIENTS

2 tbsp olive oil

1 onion, finely chopped

4 garlic cloves, finely chopped

450 g/1 lb tomatoes, peeled and roughly chopped

1.5 litres/2¾ pints vegetable stock (see page 244)

125 g/4½ oz Arborio or carnaroli rice

¼ tsp ground cumin

¼ tsp ground coriander

fresh coriander

fresh parsley sprigs, to garnish

salt and freshly ground black pepper

# Tomato Soup with Rice Ⓥ

This satisfying soup is very easy to prepar – if you're in a hurry, you can used canne tomatoes instead of fresh.

## METHOD

Heat the oil in a large saucepan over a low heat. Add the onio and garlic and cook for 5 minutes, or until softened but not browned.

Add the tomatoes, stock, rice, cumin, ground coriander and fresh coriander and season to taste with salt and pepper. Increase the heat and bring to the boil, then reduce the heat and simmer for 15–20 minutes, or until the rice is tender.

Ladle into warmed bowls, garnish with parsley and serve immediately.

**SERVES 6**

# CHILLED
Chilled Soups

## INGREDIENTS

55 g/2 oz butter
450 g/1 lb leeks,
white parts only,
thinly sliced
4 shallots, finely
sliced
250 g/9 oz potatoes,
peeled and diced
1 litre/1¾ pints
chicken stock (see
page 246)
300 ml/10 fl oz
double cream
lemon juice, to taste
salt and freshly
ground black pepper
snipped fresh chives,
to garnish

# Vichyssoise

This classic in the chilled soups repertoire
dates from the 1920s; its invention raised
the humble potato to new heights of
sophistication.

## METHOD

Heat the butter in a large saucepan over a low heat until
melted. Add the leeks and shallots, cover and cook for 5
minutes until softened but not browned.

Add the potatoes and cook, stirring occasionally, for 2–3
minutes, then add the stock and salt and pepper to taste.
Increase the heat and bring to the boil, then reduce the heat
and simmer for 15 minutes, or until the potatoes are soft.

Transfer to the bowl of a food processor and process until
smooth. Pass the soup through a sieve into a large bowl and stir
in the cream.

Cover with clingfilm and chill in the refrigerator for 4 hours.
Add a little lemon juice, then ladle into chilled bowls, garnish
with chives and serve immediately.

SERVES 4–6

## INGREDIENTS

700 g/1 lb 9 oz ripe tomatoes, peeled and deseeded

½ cucumber, peeled and chopped

3 spring onions, chopped

2 garlic cloves, very finely chopped

1 red pepper, cored, deseeded and chopped

1 tbsp chopped fresh basil

4 tbsp extra virgin olive oil

1½ tbsp red wine vinegar

salt and freshly ground black pepper

ice cubes, to serve

garlic croûtons (see page 224) and diced cucumber, to garnish

**SERVES 6**

# Gazpacho Ⓥ

None of the ingredients in this classic Spanish soup is cooked, so it has a very fresh flavour. Only full-flavoured tomatoes will work.

## METHOD

Chop the tomatoes and put into the bowl of a food processor with the remaining ingredients and some salt and pepper to taste, then process until smooth. If the soup is too thick, add little cold water.

Transfer to a large bowl, cover with clingfilm and chill in the refrigerator for at least 4 hours.

Ladle into chilled bowls, add some ice cubes, then garnish with garlic croûtons and cucumber and serve immediately.

## INGREDIENTS

2 red peppers, quartered and deseeded

3 tbsp olive oil

1 onion, very finely chopped

2 garlic cloves, very finely chopped

650 g/1 lb 7 oz ripe tomatoes, peeled and cut into chunks

150 ml/5 fl oz red wine

600 ml/1 pint vegetable stock

salt and freshly ground black pepper

garlic croûtons (see page 224) and snipped fresh chives, to garnish

# Tomato & Red Pepper Soup ⓥ

This soup is not unlike gazpacho, but the cooked vegetables bring an extra depth o flavour.

## METHOD

Place the peppers skin-side up on a grill tray and cook under a hot grill until the skins have charred. When cool enough to handle, put them into a polythene bag and rub the charred skins off. Rinse the flesh under cold water and chop.

Heat the oil in a large saucepan over a low heat, add the onio and garlic and cook for 5 minutes, or until softened but not browned. Add the peppers and tomatoes, cover and cook for minutes. Add the wine and cook for a further 5 minutes.

Add the stock and salt and pepper to taste, increase the heat and bring to the boil, then reduce the heat and simmer for 20 minutes.

Transfer to the bowl of a food processor and process until smooth. Pour into a large bowl, leave to cool, then chill in the refrigerator for at least 4 hours.

Ladle into chilled bowls, garnish with garlic croûtons and chiv and serve immediately.

SERVES 6

## INGREDIENTS

350 g/12 oz cooked
beetroot, chopped
juice and grated rind
of 1 orange
450 g/1 lb natural
Greek-style yogurt
600 ml/1 pint
unsweetened
cranberry juice
dash of Tabasco
salt and freshly
ground black pepper
caster sugar, to tase
fresh mint sprigs, to
garnish

# Summer Borscht

This soup is traditional in Russia, Poland
and the Ukraine, where it is often made
with beef and can be served hot or cold.
This chilled version is a perfect vegetarian
starter for a summer dinner party.

## METHOD

Put the beetroot into the bowl of a food processor with the
orange juice and rind, yogurt and half the cranberry juice.
Process until smooth, then press through a non-metallic sieve
into a large bowl.

Add the remaining cranberry juice and the Tabasco and season
to taste with salt and pepper. Add a little sugar to taste if the
soup is too tart. Chill in the refrigerator for 2–3 hours.

Ladle into chilled bowls, garnish with mint sprigs and serve
immediately.

**SERVES 4**

## INGREDIENTS

3 large very ripe avocados

5 spring onions, white parts only, roughly chopped

2 garlic cloves, finely chopped

juice of 1 lemon

pinch of ground cumin

pinch of paprika

450 ml/16 fl oz vegetable stock (see page 244)

300 ml/20 fl oz iced water

salt and freshly ground black pepper

chopped avocado, to garnish

# Spiced Avocado Soup Ⓥ

This deliciously creamy Spanish soup is a summer meal in a bowl. The addition of some mild spices adds a little punch.

## METHOD

Peel and stone the avocados and cut into large chunks. Place in the bowl of a food processor with the spring onions, garlic, lemon juice, cumin, paprika and salt and pepper to taste. Process until smooth.

Add the stock, in batches, and pulse to combine. Transfer to a large bowl and chill in the refrigerator for 2–3 hours.

Stir in the water and season to taste with salt and pepper, the ladle into chilled bowls, garnish with chopped avocado and serve immediately.

**SERVES 4**

## INGREDIENTS

1 large cucumber
2 garlic cloves, very finely chopped
150 ml/5 fl oz natural yogurt
300 ml/10 fl oz single cream
2 tbsp white wine vinegar
1 tbsp chopped fresh mint
salt and freshly ground black pepper
fresh mint sprigs and thinly sliced cucumber, to garnish

# Yogurt & Cucumber Soup

Yogurt, cucumber and mint are often combined in Middle-Eastern dishes and are believed to have a cooling effect.

## METHOD

Coarsely grate the unpeeled cucumber into a large bowl. Add the garlic, yogurt, cream, vinegar and mint. Season to taste with salt and pepper and stir to combine.

Cover the bowl with clingfilm and chill in the refrigerator for 2–3 hours.

Stir well, ladle into chilled bowls, garnish with mint sprigs and cucumber slices and serve immediately.

SERVES 4

## INGREDIENTS

900 g/2 lb fresh
asparagus, spears
and stalks separated
4 tbsp extra virgin
olive oil
175 g/6 oz leeks,
finely sliced
3 tbsp plain flour
1.5 litres/2¾ pints
chicken stock (see
page 246)
125 ml/4 fl oz single
cream, plus extra to
serve
1 tbsp chopped fresh
French tarragon
salt and freshly
ground black pepper

# Asparagus Soup

This light, delicately coloured soup make
the most of the short asparagus season.
The asparagus should be very fresh.

## METHOD

Bring a saucepan of water to the boil, add the asparagus spear
and blanch for 5 minutes, or until tender. Chop roughly and s
aside until needed.

Trim the asparagus stalks and chop into short pieces. Heat
the oil in a heavy-based saucepan over a medium heat, add
the leeks and cook for 5 minutes, or until softened. Add the
asparagus stalks, cover and cook for 6–7 minutes, or until
tender.

Add the flour and stir well. Cook for a further 3 minutes,
uncovered, stirring occasionally.

Add the stock, bring to the boil, stirring, then reduce the heat
to low and simmer for 30 minutes. Season to taste with salt a
pepper.

Pour the soup into the bowl of a food processor and process
until smooth, then pass through a sieve into a large bowl.

Stir in the reserved asparagus tips, the cream and the tarrago
and chill in the refrigerator for 4 hours.

Stir the soup and ladle into chilled bowls. Add a swirl of crean
to each and serve immediately.

SERVES 6

## INGREDIENTS

55 g/2 oz butter
4 spring onions,
finely sliced
1 tbsp chopped fresh
mint
450 g/1 lb fresh
peas
600 ml/1 pint
vegetable stock (see
page 244)
600 ml/1 pint milk
salt and freshly
ground black pepper
single cream and
fresh mint sprigs, to
garnish

# Fresh Pea Soup with Mint

Nothing says summer quite like the
flavour of fresh peas. Cooling mint is a
natural addition to this vibrant soup.

## METHOD

Melt the butter in a large saucepan over a medium heat. Add
the spring onions and cook until softened. Stir in the peas, m
and stock and bring to the boil, then reduce the heat, cover a
simmer for 30 minutes.

Pour the soup into the bowl of a food processor, add the mil
and salt and pepper to taste and process until smooth. Trans
to a large bowl and chill in the refrigerator for 4 hours.

Ladle the soup into chilled bowls, garnish with cream and m
sprigs and serve immediately.

SERVES 4

## INGREDIENTS

2 sweet melons,
such as honeydew,
halved, deseeded
and peeled
175 ml/6 fl oz water
85 g/3 oz caster
sugar
finely grated rind
and juice of 1 lime
fresh mint leaves, to
garnish

# Melon Soup Ⓥ

This sweet soup can be served as a
refreshing starter, or as a palate cleanser
after a rich main course.

## METHOD

Using a melon baller, scoop out 24 melon balls and set aside.
Chop the remaining melon flesh and place it in the bowl of a
food processor.

Put the water into a small saucepan, add the sugar and lime
rind, bring to the boil, then simmer for 2–3 minutes. Set aside
and leave to cool, then add the syrup and lime juice to the
melon flesh and process until smooth.

Pour the soup into a large bowl, stir in the chopped basil and
chill in the refrigerator for 4 hours.

Ladle the soup into chilled bowls, garnish with mint leaves and
the reserved melon balls and serve immediately.

**SERVES 4-6**

## INGREDIENTS

500 g/1 lb 2 oz
sorrel leaves

1 onion, thinly sliced

1.5 litres/2¾ pints
vegetable stock (see
page 244)

2 tbsp sugar

4 tbsp lemon juice

2 eggs

150 ml/5 fl oz
soured cream

salt

sliced spring onions,
to garnish

# Sorrel Soup

This is an unusual soup with a distinctive
bite. Sorrel can be cultivated but can also
be found growing wild.

## METHOD

Put the sorrel into a large saucepan with the onion and stock
Bring to the boil, then reduce the heat and simmer for 10
minutes.

Add the sugar and half the lemon juice to the pan, stir to
combine, then simmer for a further 10 minutes.

Meanwhile, put the eggs and soured cream into a large bowl
and beat well together. Slowly add 250 ml/8 fl oz of the hot
mixture, whisking lightly to avoid curdling. Add another 250
ml/8 fl oz of the hot mixture in the same way.

Add the egg mixture to the saucepan, stirring constantly to
avoid curdling. Cook for several minutes over a very low heat
until the soup has thickened a little. Season to taste with salt
and add the remaining lemon juice.

Remove from the heat and leave to cool, then chill in the
refrigerator for 2–4 hours. Serve in chilled bowls, garnished
with spring onions.

**SERVES 4–6**

# DINNER PARTY

Dinner Party Soups

## INGREDIENTS

25 g/1 oz butter

3 spring onions, very finely chopped

3 garlic cloves, very finely chopped

1 large cucumber, peeled, deseeded and diced

300 ml/10 fl oz milk

250 g/9 oz cooked peeled prawns or crayfish

1 tbsp chopped fresh dill

1 tbsp chopped fresh mint

300 ml/10 fl oz single cream

salt and freshly ground black pepper

fresh dill sprigs and chilli oil, to garnish

# Cucumber Soup with Prawns

This impressive soup is very simple to prepare. It's best served chilled, so it can be prepared ahead.

## METHOD

Heat the butter in a large saucepan over a low heat until melted. Add the spring onions and garlic and cook for 3–4 minutes, or until softened but not browned. Add the cucumber and cook, stirring, for 2 minutes, or until tender.

Add the milk, increase the heat to medium and bring just to boiling point, then reduce the heat and simmer for 5 minutes.

Transfer the soup to the bowl of a food processor and process until smooth. Season to taste with salt and pepper, transfer to a bowl and leave to cool.

Stir in the prawns, dill, mint and cream, cover the bowl with clingfilm and chill in the refrigerator for at least 2 hours.

Serve in chilled bowls, garnished with dill sprigs and chilli oil.

**SERVES 4**

## INGREDIENTS

850 ml/1½ pints chicken stock (see page 246)

55 g/2 oz long-grain rice

3 large egg yolks

4 tbsp lemon juice, or to taste

3 tbsp chopped fresh parsley

salt and freshly ground black pepper

lemon slices and fresh parsley sprigs, to garnish

# Egg & Lemon Soup

This classic Greek soup takes less than half an hour to prepare, but it has to be served immediately – the eggs will curdle if it's reheated.

## METHOD

Bring the stock just to simmering in a large saucepan. Add the rice, then partially cover and cook for 10 minutes, or until the rice is just tender, but still firm to the bite. Season to taste with salt and pepper.

Meanwhile, whisk the egg yolks, then gradually add the lemon juice, whisking until light and frothy. Add a ladleful of the hot stock and whisk again.

Remove the soup from the heat and slowly whisk in the egg and lemon mixture until it thickens slightly.

Stir in the parsley and serve immediately, garnished with lemon slices and parsley sprigs.

SERVES 4-6

## INGREDIENTS

25 g/1 oz butter

1 leek, finely sliced

1 garlic clove, very finely chopped

450 g/1 lb frozen peas

1.2 litres/2 pints ham stock (see page 250)

1 tbsp snipped fresh chives, plus extra to garnish

300 ml/10 fl oz double cream

6 tbsp crème fraîche

4 slices Parma ham, roughly torn

salt and freshly ground black pepper

# Green Pea Soup with Parma Ham

This easy chilled soup made with frozen peas is served with crème fraîche and Parma ham.

## METHOD

Heat the butter in a large saucepan over a low heat until melted. Add the leek and garlic and cook for 5 minutes, or until softened but not browned.

Add the peas, stock and chives and bring to the boil.

Transfer the soup to the bowl of a food processor and process until smooth. Pour into a large bowl, add the cream and salt and pepper to taste and stir to combine. Chill in the refrigerator for at least 2 hours.

Ladle the soup into chilled bowls, add 1 tablespoon of crème fraîche and a few pieces of Parma ham to each portion, then scatter over some chives and serve.

SERVES 6

## INGREDIENTS

2 tbsp vegetable oil

1 onion, finely chopped

3 Williams pears, peeled, cored and roughly chopped

400 ml/14 fl oz vegetable stock (see page 244)

juice of 1 lemon

175 g/6 oz Stilton cheese, crumbled

salt and freshly ground black pepper

paprika and fresh parsley sprigs, to garnish

# Pear & Stilton Soup

The classic combination of pears and blue cheese works surprisingly well in this unusual soup.

## METHOD

Heat the oil in a large saucepan over a low heat. Add the onion and cook for 5 minutes, or until softened but not browned.

Add the pears and the stock, increase the heat and bring to the boil. Reduce the heat and cook for 8 minutes, or until the pears are soft, then add the lemon juice and cheese and season to taste with salt and pepper.

Transfer the soup to the bowl of a food processor and process until smooth, then pass it through a sieve and return to the saucepan. Reheat the soup over a low heat. Do not boil.

Ladle into warmed bowls, garnish with a dusting of paprika and some parsley sprigs and serve immediately.

**SERVES 6**

## INGREDIENTS

4 tbsp olive oil

400 g/14 oz sorrel leaves, stalks removed

1 small onion, finely chopped

1 shallot, finely chopped

450 g/1 lb potatoes, diced

1 litre/1¾ pints vegetable stock (see page 244)

salt and freshly ground black pepper

single cream and croûtons (see page 224), to garnish

# Potato & Sorrel Soup

This fresh-tasting vibrant green soup makes a perfect starter for a summer dinner party.

## METHOD

Heat the oil in a large saucepan over a low heat. Add the sorre cover and heat until wilted. Add the onion and shallot and co for 1–2 minutes.

Add the potatoes and stock, increase the heat and bring to the boil, then reduce the heat and simmer for 30–40 minutes, un the potatoes are tender.

Transfer the soup to the bowl of a food processor and process until smooth, then return to the saucepan and reheat over a low heat. Do not boil.

Ladle into warmed bowls, garnish with cream and croûtons a serve immediately.

**SERVES 4**

# Watercress Soup

**This fresh-tasting soup has a lovely citrus hint. It can be served hot or cold.**

**INGREDIENTS**

1 tbsp olive oil

1 large onion, finely chopped

200 g/7 oz watercress

600 ml/1 pint vegetable stock (see page 244)

juice and grated rind of 1 large orange

2 tsp cornflour

150 ml/5 fl oz single cream

salt and freshly ground black pepper

fresh parsley sprigs, to garnish

## METHOD

Heat the oil in a large saucepan over a low heat. Add the onion and cook for 5 minutes, or until softened but not browned. Add the watercress, cover and cook for 5 minutes.

Add the stock with the orange juice and rind, increase the heat and bring to the boil, then reduce the heat and simmer for 15 minutes.

Transfer the soup to the bowl of a food processor and process until smooth, then pass it through a sieve and return to the saucepan.

Blend the cornflour with a little cream, then stir into the soup. Add the remaining cream, season to taste with salt and pepper and bring to the boil, stirring frequently.

Ladle into warmed bowls, garnish with parsley and serve immediately.

**SERVES 4**

## INGREDIENTS

25 g/1 oz butter

1 onion, very finely
chopped

450 g/1 lb mixed
mushrooms, finely
chopped

300 ml/10 fl oz
vegetable stock (see
page 244)

300 ml/10 fl oz
single cream

2 tbsp chopped fresh
tarragon

salt and freshly
ground black pepper

fresh tarragon sprigs,
to garnish

# Mushroom Soup with Tarragon

If you can get it, use French tarragon for
this creamy soup – the flavour is very
subtle.

## METHOD

Heat the butter in a large saucepan over a low heat until
melted. Add the onion and cook for 5 minutes, or until
softened but not browned. Add the mushrooms and cook,
stirring, for 3–4 minutes.

Stir in the stock and cream, increase the heat and bring to the
boil. Reduce the heat and simmer for 20 minutes, or until the
mushrooms are tender.

Add the tarragon and season to taste with salt and pepper,
then transfer to the bowl of a food processor and process unti
smooth. Return the soup to the saucepan and reheat over a lo
heat. Do not boil.

Ladle the soup into warmed bowls, garnish with pepper and
tarragon sprigs and serve immediately.

**SERVES 6**

## INGREDIENTS

50 g/1¾ oz butter
2 large Spanish
onions, thinly sliced
1 garlic clove, very
finely chopped
12 saffron threads
55 g/2 oz toasted
ground almonds
700 ml/1¼ pints
vegetable stock (see
page 244)
3 tbsp dry sherry
salt and freshly
ground black pepper
chopped fresh
parsley and toasted
flaked almonds, to
garnish

# Onion & Almond Soup with Sherry

This unusual Spanish soup gets its lovely colour from saffron. The sherry adds a touch of warmth and sweetness.

## METHOD

Heat the butter in a large saucepan over a low heat until melted. Add the onions and garlic and cook for 15–20 minute stirring frequently, until the onions are softened but not browned.

Add the saffron and cook for 3 minutes, then add the almond and cook, stirring, for a further 3 minutes. Add the stock and sherry and season to taste with salt and pepper. Increase the heat and bring to the boil, then reduce the heat and simmer f 10 minutes.

Transfer the soup to the bowl of a food processor and process until smooth. Return to the saucepan and reheat over a low heat. Do not boil.

Ladle into warmed bowls, garnish with parsley and flaked almonds and serve immediately.

**SERVES 6**

## INGREDIENTS

600 g/1 lb 5 oz cooked prawns in their shells

4 tbsp olive oil

1 large onion, finely chopped

1 carrot, finely chopped

1 fennel bulb, chopped

4 tbsp dry white wine

4 tbsp brandy

400 g/14 oz canned chopped tomatoes

1 litre/1¾ pints fish stock (see page 248)

1 tsp lemon juice

25 g/1 oz butter

double cream and fresh flatleaf parsley sprigs, to garnish

# Prawn Bisque

A bisque is a strained soup, with shellfish as the main ingredient. The prawn shells enhance the flavour.

## METHOD

Shell the prawns and set aside until needed. Put the shells into a large saucepan with the oil and fry for 5 minutes. Add the onion, carrot and fennel and cook for 10 minutes, or until the vegetables are softened but not browned.

Add the wine and brandy, bubble over a high heat for 1 minute, then add the tomatoes, stock and lemon juice. Cover and simmer for 30 minutes.

Meanwhile, chop the prawns into small pieces, reserving a few whole prawns to garnish. Put the butter into a small frying pan and heat over a medium heat until melted. Add the chopped prawns and fry for 2 minutes. Set aside until needed.

Transfer the soup to the bowl of a food processor and pulse until the shells are finely chopped. Press through a sieve into a clean saucepan and cook over a low heat for 10 minutes. Add the prawns and stir.

Ladle the soup into warmed bowls, garnish with cream, the reserved whole prawns and some parsley and serve immediately.

**SERVES 6**

## INGREDIENTS

225 ml/8 fl oz fish stock (see page 248)
1 small white onion, diced
1 celery stick, diced
125 ml/4 fl oz Irish stout
450 g/1 lb potatoes, diced
1 tsp fresh thyme
24 fresh shucked oysters
125 ml/4 fl oz milk
freshly ground black pepper
chopped fresh watercress or parsley, to garnish

# Creamy Oyster Bisque

This rich and luxurious soup combines two favourite Irish ingredients, oysters and stout.

## METHOD

Heat 2 tablespoons of the stock in a large saucepan. Add the onion and celery and cook over a medium heat until translucent. Add the stout with the remaining stock, then add the potatoes and thyme, bring to the boil and cook until the potatoes are softened.

Transfer to the bowl of a food processor, add half the oysters, the milk and pepper to taste and process until smooth.

Return to the pan and cook over a medium heat until the oysters are cooked through. Do not boil.

Serve in warmed bowls, garnished with the remaining oysters and some watercress or parsley.

**SERVES 4-6**

ACCOMPANIMENTS

## INGREDIENTS

4 tbsp olive oil
4 thick slices bread, cubed

# Croûtons

These will liven up any soup. Keep an eye on them while they're baking as they will burn easily.

## METHOD

Preheat the oven to 180°C/350°F/Gas Mark 4.

Heat the oil in a large frying pan over a medium heat. Add the bread cubes, tossing to coat in the oil.

Spread the cubes on a baking tray in a single layer and bake in the preheated oven for 15 minutes until crisp and dry.

Variation: If you prefer garlic croûtons, sauté a finely chopped garlic clove in the oil for 4 minutes before adding the bread cubes.

SERVES 6–8

## INGREDIENTS

450 g/1 lb plain white flour, plus extra for dusting

1 tsp salt

1 tsp bicarbonate of soda

400 ml/14 fl oz buttermilk

# White Soda Bread

Soda bread, served with lots of butter, is a great accompaniment to hearty winter soups.

## METHOD

Preheat the oven to 230°C/450°F/Gas Mark 8. Dust a baking sheet with flour.

Mix the dry ingredients in a large mixing bowl, then make a well in the centre and gradually add the buttermilk, drawing the dry ingredients from the side of the bowl. Mix until a mo dough forms.

Turn the dough out onto a floured work surface and shape it into a round about 5 cm/2 inches high. Place the round on th prepared baking sheet and use a floured knife to cut a deep cross in it.

Bake in the preheated oven for 30–45 minutes until the loaf sounds hollow when tapped on the base.

**MAKES 1 LOAF**

## INGREDIENTS

675 g/1 lb 8 oz
wholemeal flour

450 g/1 lb strong
white flour, plus
extra for dusting

2 tsp bicarbonate
of soda

2 tsp salt

850 ml/1½ pints
buttermilk, plus extra
if needed

# Brown Soda Bread

This textured bread is the perfect
accompaniment to almost any dish,
especially soup.

## METHOD

Preheat the oven to 230°C/450°F/Gas Mark 8. Dust a large
baking sheet with flour.

Mix the dry ingredients in a large mixing bowl, then make a
well in the centre and gradually add the buttermilk, drawing
the dry ingredients from the sides of the bowl. Mix until a soft
dough forms, adding more buttermilk if necessary. The dough
should not be too moist.

Turn out the dough onto a floured work surface, divide into
two pieces and shape both pieces into a round about 5 cm/2
inches high. Place on the prepared baking sheet and use a
floured knife to cut a deep cross in each loaf.

Bake in the preheated oven for 15–20 minutes, then reduce
the oven temperature to 200°C/400°F/Gas Mark 6 and bake for
a further 20–25 minutes until the loaves sound hollow when
tapped on the base.

**MAKES 2 LOAVES**

## INGREDIENTS

vegetable oil, for
greasing
1.3 kg/3 lb
wholemeal flour
500 ml/18 fl oz
500 ml/18 fl oz milk
water
1 tbsp soft light
brown sugar
55 g/2 oz fresh
yeast
2 tsp salt
milk, for brushing

# Brown Bread

This nutty yeast bread has a slightly sweet
flavour. It's well worth taking the time
needed to prepare it with fresh yeast.

## METHOD

Grease two 900-g/2-lb loaf tins and the inside of two large
polythene bags.

Put half the flour into a large mixing bowl. Mix the milk and
water together in a jug, then add the sugar and yeast. Add to the
flour and beat well. Cover the bowl with a damp tea towel and
leave to stand for 10–15 minutes until the mixture is frothy.

Add the remaining flour and the salt and mix to a soft dough.
Knead for 10 minutes.

Divide the dough into two pieces and place a piece in each
of the prepared tins. Put the tins into the prepared bags and
leave to stand until the dough has risen to the top of the tins.
Meanwhile, preheat the oven to 230°C/450°F/Gas Mark 8.

Brush the tops of the loaves with milk and bake in the
preheated oven for 30–40 minutes until risen and golden
brown and they sound hollow when tapped on the base. Leave
to cool in the tins for 10 minutes, the transfer to a wire rack and
leave to cool completely.

**MAKES 2 LOAVES**

## INGREDIENTS

175 g/6 oz
wholemeal flour,
plus extra for dusting

175 g/6 oz plain
flour

½ tsp salt

1 tsp bicarbonate
of soda

55 g/2 oz butter

1 tbsp soft light
brown sugar

200 ml/7 fl oz
buttermilk

1 egg, beaten, for
glazing

# Wholemeal Scones

A hearty scone that goes well with cheesy soups.

## METHOD

Preheat the oven to 200°C/400°F/Gas Mark 6. Dust a baking sheet with flour.

Put the wholemeal flour, plain flour, salt and bicarbonate of soda into a bowl and mix to combine. Add the butter and rub it in with your fingertips until fine crumbs form. Add the sugar and mix to combine.

Stir in enough buttermilk to make a soft dough. Turn out onto a surface lightly dusted with flour and knead for about 10 seconds.

Press out the dough to a thickness of 4 cm/1½ inches, then use a 6-cm/2½-inch round biscuit cutter to cut out 8–10 rounds, reshaping the trimmings as necessary.

Place the scones on the prepared baking sheet, then brush with the beaten egg and bake in the preheated oven for 15 minutes or until risen and golden. Transfer to a wire rack and leave to cool slightly. Serve warm.

**MAKES 8–10**

## INGREDIENTS

225 g/8 oz plain white flour, plus extra for dusting

1 heaped tsp baking powder

55 g/2 oz butter, plus extra for greasing

100 g/3½ oz mature Cheddar cheese, grated

1 tsp English mustard powder

100 ml/3½ fl oz milk, plus extra for brushing

salt and freshly ground black pepper

# Cheese Scones

These are delicious served with winter soups. Use a really mature Cheddar chees for the best flavour.

## METHOD

Preheat the oven to 230°C/450°F/Gas Mark 8. Grease a baking sheet.

Sift the flour and baking powder into a mixing bowl, then cut the butter and rub in until fine crumbs form. Mix in the chees and mustard, adding salt and pepper to taste.

Make a well in the centre of the dry ingredients and add the milk, mixing to a soft dough. Turn out the dough onto a work surface lightly dusted with flour and roll out to thickness of 2 cm/¾ inch.

Using a lightly floured fluted round cutter, cut out 10 scones and place them on the prepared baking sheet. Brush with mil and bake in the preheated oven for 10–15 minutes, or until well-risen and golden. Eat on the day of baking.

MAKES 10

## INGREDIENTS

100 g/3½ oz plain
flour, plus extra for
dusting
1 tsp baking powder
large pinch of salt
55 g/2 oz butter,
plus extra for
greasing
4 tbsp mashed
potatoes
milk, for mixing and
brushing
butter, to serve

# Potato Scones

Just a small amount of leftover potato
gives these scones a hearty texture and
flavour. They're great with chunky winter
soups.

## METHOD

Preheat the oven to 180°C/350°F/Gas Mark 4. Grease a baking
tray.

Sift the flour, baking powder and salt together into a bowl, the
rub in the butter. Add the potatoes and a little milk and mix
until a soft dough forms.

Turn out the dough onto a floured work surface and roll out
to thickness of 2 cm/¾ inch. Use a floured cutter to cut out
rounds, then place them on the prepared tray.

Brush the tops with milk and bake in the preheated oven for
about 15 minutes until golden brown. Serve warm with butter.

**MAKES ABOUT 6**

## INGREDIENTS

225 g/8 oz butter, melted and cooled
1 sachet dried yeast
125 ml/4 fl oz lukewarm water
100 g/3½ oz sugar
500 ml/16 fl oz milk
2 large eggs, beaten
1 tbsp salt
1.5 kg/3 lb 5 oz plain flour, plus extra for dusting

# Parker House Rolls

## These soft rolls originate in the United States, and are popular at dinner parties.

## METHOD

Brush a large bowl with a little butter and line two baking sheets with baking paper. Mix the yeast with the water and 1 teaspoon of the sugar in the bowl of a stand mixer. Leave to stand for 10 minutes, or until it foams.

Beat in the remaining sugar, 175 g/6 oz of the butter, the milk, eggs and salt. Replace the whisk with the dough hook, then gradually add the flour, beating at a low speed, until the dough comes together, then increase the speed to medium and beat until the dough forms a ball around the hook.

Transfer the dough to the prepared bowl, cover with clingfilm and leave to stand in a warm place for 1½ hours, or until doubled in size.

Preheat the oven to 190°C/375°F/Gas Mark 5. Transfer the dough to a lightly floured work surface and shape into a 23 x 40-cm/9 x 16-inch rectangle. Use a floured knife to cut the dough into 3 strips lengthwise, then cut each strip into 12 small strips widthwise. Fold each strip and place, seam-side down, on one of the prepared baking sheets, until you have two rows of 18 rolls each on both sheets. The rolls in each row should be just touching each other, but you should leave about 10 cm/4 inches between the rows.

Bake the rolls in the preheated oven for 18 minutes, until browned, then remove from the oven and brush with the remaining butter. Transfer to a wire rack and leave to cool.

**MAKES 36**

## INGREDIENTS

55 g/2 oz fresh basil
leaves
70 g/2¼ oz freshly
grated Parmesan
cheese
2 garlic cloves,
roughly chopped
15 g/½ oz pine nuts
pinch of salt
125 ml/4 fl oz extra-
virgin olive oil

# Pesto

This uncooked green sauce is
very versatile, and is a handy soup
accompaniment, swirled in for extra
flavour just before serving.

## METHOD

Put all the ingredients except the oil into the bowl of a food
processor and process for 1 minute. Gradually add the oil,
pulsing between each addition.

Process until a smooth sauce forms.

Transfer to a covered container and keep in the refrigerator for
2–3 days.

**MAKES 6
SERVINGS**

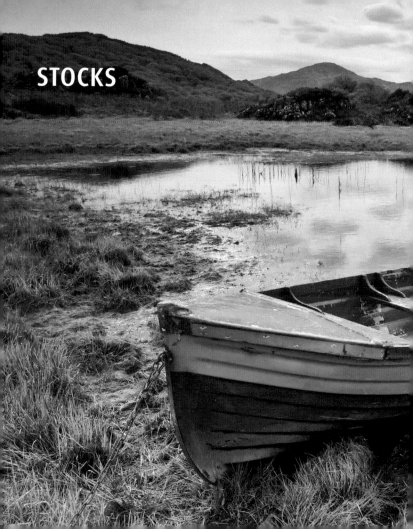

STOCKS

## INGREDIENTS

1 tbsp olive oil
1 onion, chopped
2 celery sticks, chopped
2 carrots, cut up
5 spring onions, chopped
8 garlic cloves, finely chopped
8 fresh parsley sprigs
8 fresh thyme sprigs
2 bay leaves
1 tsp salt
2.5 litres water

# Vegetable Stock 🅥

A basic vegetable stock is simplicity itself to prepare and can be used in any soup. If you don't have all the ingredients listed you can use any vegetables, even potato peelings.

## METHOD

Heat the oil in a stockpot over a high heat, then add the vegetables and herbs and cook for 5–10 minutes, stirring frequently.

Add the salt and water and bring to the boil. Reduce the heat and simmer for about 30 minutes.

Strain into a bowl or jug, discarding the vegetables, and leave cool. The stock can be kept in the refrigerator for several days or can be frozen for up to 1 month.

**MAKES ABOUT 2 LITRES/3½ PINTS**

## INGREDIENTS

450 g/1 lb chicken
pieces
1 onion, chopped
3 celery sticks,
chopped
2 carrots, chopped
1½ tsp salt
3 cloves
1.5 litres/2¼ pints
water

# Chicken Stock

Chicken stock adds an extra depth of
flavour to most vegetable soups and is
essential in chicken based-soups.
You can use a leftover chicken carcass if
you have one.

## METHOD

Put all the ingredients into a stockpot and bring to the boil o
a high heat. Reduce the heat and simmer for 1 hour.

Strain the stock into a bowl or jug, discarding the chicken an
vegetables, and skim any fat off the surface. Leave to cool.

The stock can be kept in the refrigerator for 2–3 days, or can
frozen for up to 1 month.

**MAKES ABOUT 1.2
LITRES/2 PINTS**

## INGREDIENTS

1 tbsp olive oil
1 onion, chopped
1 kg/2 lb 4 oz white
fish trimmings,
heads and bones
250 ml/9 fl oz dry
white wine
1 litre/1¾ pints
water
2 fresh parsley sprigs
2 fresh thyme sprigs
1 bay leaf
pinch of salt

# Fish Stock

If you worry that fish stock is complicate
to prepare, this simple version will chang
your mind. Your fishmonger will be able
to supply the fish trimmings.

## METHOD

Heat the oil in a large stockpot over a medium heat, then add
the onion and cook for 3 minutes.

Add the fish and cook, stirring occasionally, for a further 5
minutes, then add the wine, water, herbs and salt. Bring to
the boil, then reduce the heat and simmer for 30 minutes,
skimming off any scum that rises to the surface.

Strain the stock into a bowl or jug, discarding the fish and
vegetables, and leave to cool.

The stock can be kept in the refrigerator for up to 1 week, or
can be frozen for up to 1 month.

**MAKES ABOUT 1.2
LITRES/2 PINTS**

## INGREDIENTS

1 meaty ham bone
1 onion, chopped
2 celery sticks,
chopped
2 carrots, chopped
1 leek, chopped
6 whole black
peppercorns
5 fresh parsley sprigs
2 fresh thyme sprigs
1 bay leaf
2 litres/3½ pints
water

# Ham Stock

This stock makes good use of the bone left over from a baked or boiled ham, an provides the perfect base for pea or bear soups.

## METHOD

Put all the ingredients into a stockpot and bring to the boil o a medium heat, then reduce the heat and simmer for 2 hour skimming any scum that rises to the surface.

Remove from the heat and strain into a bowl or jug, discardi the bone and vegetables.

This stock can be kept in the refrigerator for up to 1 week, o can be frozen for up to 1 month.

**MAKES ABOUT 2
LITRES/3½ PINTS**

## INGREDIENTS

2.5 kg/5 lb 8 oz
beef bones
3 onions, halved
1 garlic bulb, halved
horizontally
4 litres/7 pints
water
bouquet garni
(parsley sprigs,
thyme sprigs, sage
leaves)
2 leeks, chopped
3 carrots, chopped
2 celery sticks,
chopped
1 tsp salt
1 tbsp whole black
peppercorns

**MAKES ABOUT 2
LITRES/3½ PINTS**

# Rich Beef Stock

This stock is made with roasted bones
and is reduced to half its volume during
cooking, giving it an intense flavour. If
you need something lighter, dilute it wit
some water before adding to your soup.

## METHOD

Preheat the oven to 200°C/400°F/Gas Mark 6. Put the bones
into a large roasting tin with the onions, garlic and a little wa
and roast for 45 minutes.

Add the water to a large stockpot and bring to the boil over a
medium heat. Add the contents of the roasting tin, scraping
in any browned bits from the base of the tin. Add the bouqu
garni, vegetables, salt and peppercorns. Bring back to the bo
then reduce the heat and simmer for at least 4 hours, adding
more water if necessary.

Strain into a large jug, discarding the solid ingredients, then
return to the pan and increase the heat to medium. Cook fo
1 hour, or until the liquid is reduced by half. The stock can b
kept in the refrigerator for 1 week, or can be frozen for up t
month.

Variation: Make a lamb stock by substituting the beef bones
lamb bones.

For permission to reproduce copyright photographs, the publisher gratefully acknowledges the following:

Except for Ben Potter or Alamy as noted, images courtesy of Shutterstock.

p1 Jaz1111
p3 MaraZe
p5 Bob Pool
p7 mubus7
p9 John & Penny
p12 Fabiano's
p15 Ben Potter
p17 Ben Potter
p19 Joe Gough
p21 Ben Potter
p23 Whiteaster
p25 Fanfo
p27 Aleksandra Duda
p29 Paul Cowan
p31 Foodio
p33 Robin Stewart
p34 Tanya Sid
p37 In Green
p39 Alpha_7D
p41 Evgeniya Ulanova
p43 Marta Ortiz
p45 Maria Kovaleva
p47 Ben Potter
p49 Yulia Grigoryeva
p51 Nada54
p53 Kati Finell

p55 Matt Pickett
p56 Baibaz
p59 Maria Kovaleva
p61 Martin Turzak
p63 Pingpongcat
p65 Jabiru
p67 M.Botarelli
p69 Ben Potter
p71 GreenArt
p73 Timolina
p75 Liudmyla Yaremenko
p77 Ben Potter
p78 Riccar
p81 Ben Potter
p83 Lisovskaya Natalia
p85 Dmytro Gilitukha
p87 Yulia Davidovich
p89 Ben Potter
p91 Jabiru
p93 Dar1930
p95 Ben Potter
p97 IngridHS
p99 Juefraphoto
p101 Ben Potter
p103 Piotr Krzeslak
p105 Ben Potter
p107 Rihardzz
p108 Lampas Azami
p111 Magdanatka

p113 Yuliia Kononenko
p115 Ben Potter
p117 OlegD
p119 Ben Potter
p121 Ben Potter
p123 Yuliia Kononenko
p125 Stepanek photography
p127 Ben Potter
p129 Nesavinov
p131 Anna Pustinnikova
p132 Stefania Rossitto
p135 Ben Potter
p137 Hlphoto
p139 Mahara
p141 Razmarinka
p143 Ben Potter
p145 Ben Potter
p147 Karl Allgaeuer
p149 Marco Mayer
p151 Ben Potter
p153 Ben Potter
p155 Amikphoto
p156 Dimitris K
p159 Alicja Neumiler
p161 Ben Potter
p163 Ben Potter
p165 Ben Potter

p167 Denio109
p169 Ewa Rejmer/ Alamy
p171 Art Cook Studio
p173 Ben Potter
p175 Ben Potter
p177 Aleksandra Duda
p178 Iuliia Karnaushenko
p181 Etorres
p183 Maria Kovaleva
p185 Yuliia Holovchenko
p187 Tatiana Goskova
p189 MK Photograp55
p191 Simone Voigt
p193 Nada54
p195 Nataliya Arzamasova
p197 Margouillat Photo
p199 Africa Studio
p200 Christopher Halloran
p203 Tinas Dreamworld
p205 Minadezhda
p207 Ben Potter
p209 Ben Potter

p211 Ben Potter
p213 CKP1001
p215 Steve Moss/ Alamy
p217 Travellight
p219 Alena Haurylik
p221 Ben Potter
p222 Jag Cz
p225 Alexei Logvinovich
p227 Space Monkey Pics
p229 Leigh Boardman
p231 Paul Cowan
p233 Istetiana
p235 D. Pimborough
p237 Ben Potter
p239 Ben Potter
p241 Artem Evdokimov
p242 Patryk Kosmider
p245 Ben Potter
p247 Zigzag Mountain Art
p249 Ben Potter
p251 Ben Potter
p253 Photosiber
p254 James Fraser